A LENTEN PILGRIMAGE

A Lenten Pilgrimage

Scriptural Meditations in the Holy Land

David E. Rosage

Servant Books
Ann Arbor, Michigan

copyright © 1980 by David E. Rosage

Published by Servant Books
       Box 8617
       Ann Arbor, Michigan 48107

Cover Photo © Marvin E. Newman from Woodfin
Camp and Associates.

Book Design by John B. Leidy

Printed in the United States of America

ISBN 0-89283-081-6

Scripture quotations used in this book are taken from
the *New American Bible* copyright © 1970 by the
Confraternity of Christian Doctrine, and used by
permission.

CONTENTS

WEEK FOUR

WEEK FIVE

WEEK SIX

HOLY WEEK

INTRODUCTION

One of the most basic requisites for our spiritual growth is the conviction that God really loves us personally and individually. Furthermore, we must know that he loves us just as we are: weak, indifferent, half-hearted, sinful. Intellectually we can readily accept this truth, because we can advance many cogent reasons to prove that God does love us. However, we live by our heart; we must "know with our heart" that we are loved by God. Only then will this conviction become a habitual attitude which will be transformed into a positive and operative habit pattern.

Today we are living with the risen, glorified, exalted Jesus who is enthroned at the right hand of the Father. He loves us with an infinite love. He himself said: "As the Father has loved me, so I have loved you" (Jn 15:9). We know that the Father loves the Son with an infinite love. It cannot be any greater. Jesus assures us that he loves us with that same infinite love. In his next breath, during his last discourse in the Upper Room Jesus said: "There is no greater love than this; to lay down one's life for one's friends" (Jn 15:13). The next day Jesus did exactly that. He laid down his life for us.

How vividly St. Paul describes this attitude of Jesus: "It is rare that anyone should lay down his life for a just man, though it be barely possible that for a good man someone may have the courage to die. It is precisely in this that God proved his love for us: that while we were still sinners, Christ died for us" (Rom 5:7-8). Do we need further evidence of the love which Jesus has for us?

Throughout our lifetime, and especially during the season of Lent, we strive to come to a greater appreciation of his immense love for us, and also to experience his love within us. We can strive to reach that awareness of his love by reliving the events of Jesus' passion and death with him. We do not want to relive his gruesome physical suffering: the burning pain of the scourging, the penetrating sting of the crowning with thorns, the piercing sword of rejection. These considerations could tend toward masochism. On the contrary, the sufferings of Jesus are the source of his glory. We want to be with the risen Jesus as he recalls for us, and we recall with him, the suffering and rejection which led to his glorification.

There may appear to be a sense of rejection running as a theme through the pages that make up this volume. This is not intended to be negative, but rather to prove more conclusively how much Jesus loves us. In spite of rejection, he persevered in loving us to the end. Likewise, this fact will prepare us to face the little persecutions which inevitably will be ours as we try not only to walk in the footsteps of Jesus, but also to be identified with him.

Our contemplations on the sufferings of Jesus should lead us into a greater sense of gratitude for that kind of love which Jesus has for us. His love could not be satisfied until he had given everything, even to the last drop of his blood. Time spent in contemplating the infinitely generous gift Jesus made of himself will draw us into a deep sense of gratitude and willingness to respond more graciously and generously than in the past.

As we spend time with the exalted Jesus, listening to his Word, we should be motivated by a deepening spirit of compassion. Jesus suffered for us and for all mankind. His Body is still suffering in the world today. As we ponder the generosity of Jesus in offering himself without reservation for our salvation, we are more and more inclined to spare nothing in reaching out in love to the suffering members of his Body. Likewise, we will be more receptive to whatever pain and suffering may come our way.

Jesus assures us of the infinite love which his Father has for us: "Yes, God so loved the world that he gave his only Son, that whoever believes in him may not die but have eternal life" (Jn 3:16). The Father loves us with a many-faceted love: a creating love, a providing love, a forgiving love, a healing love, an enduring love.

Jesus assured us, by his passion and death, that his love, too, is an all-embracing love. Love, by its very nature, is reciprocal. Love asks love in return. As we contemplate the love of Jesus enveloping and permeating us, we cannot help but respond to his love.

Prayer is our loving relationship with our Father. It is a gift from God. In prayer the Lord leads each one of us in a different way. However, there are some general norms of procedure which may be conducive to our living with the risen Jesus during these weeks of Lent:

1. *Enter prayer slowly.* Give yourself time to relax and set aside the preoccupations of every day.

2. *Begin reverently.* Prayer is a private audience with the Lord of heaven and earth. He is a universal God, but he is also an exclusive God. He is giving us his undivided attention. His total concern is just for us at this moment.

3. *Listen attentively.* The Father wants to communicate with us. He has been patiently and eagerly waiting for this moment when we give ourselves completely to him. Listening means being totally for God, and letting him be for us. It is putting ourselves entirely at his disposal. St. James gives us some practical, paternal advice on this matter: "Humbly welcome the word that has taken root in you, with its power to save. Act on this word. If all you do is listen to it, you are deceiving yourselves" (Jas 1:21-22).

4. *Taste and savor his Word.* As we would taste and sip a fine wine, so should we savor his Word. When we receive a letter from a person very near and dear to us, the letter really makes that person present to us. We hear the voice, we visualize him or her present before us. Jesus is even more present in his Word. We are resting in his presence.

This kind of prayer forms our heart, even though we may not be aware of its transforming power. We may not experience any great inspiration, nor any bright illumination, nor any profound or new meaning hidden in his Word.

Quietly and unobtrusively his Word molds, shapes and transforms our heart. It makes our attitude more Christ-like, which in turn forms genuine Christian habit patterns within us. These, then, become the norms of our daily living.

As these habit patterns become the guidelines of our daily living, we will be responding with greater gratitude, a more compassionate concern for others, and a deeper love for God and for our brothers and sisters.

To reach this plateau in our prayer, and to use this manual more effectively as a stepping-stone into deeper prayer, it would be well to:

1. First read the scriptural passage suggested for each day's prayer.
2. Read it slowly, reflectively, prayerfully, letting each word find a home in your heart.
3. Read the commentary as an auxiliary to prayer.
4. Return to the scriptural passage, ponder it, rest with it, pray with it, as you rest in the presence of the Lord.

Recently I was privileged to spend some time in the Holy Land. I was invited by the Sisters of the Holy Cross, from Notre Dame, Indiana, to be a part of the renewal team at their Mater Ecclesiae Center in Tiberias, Israel. For some years the Sisters of the Holy Cross have successfully offered and conducted a spiritual renewal program at their Center in the Holy Land. They offer a twofold program each year: the first for native sisters from Africa and Asia, and the second for missionary sisters who are laboring in the mission fields of Africa and Asia.

I had the joy of working with the second group, the missionary sisters. After a seminar on prayer, spiritual direction, and discernment, and before the thirty-day retreat began, we made a two-week pilgrimage to Jerusalem. Together we visited the Holy Places which are sacred to all Christians because Jesus sanctified them by his human and divine presence.

We journeyed to these sacred places to spend time in prayer and contemplation. At many of these shrines we had the privilege of offering the Eucharist together. Certainly, it was a unique experience for all of us. The eucharistic presence of Jesus helped us relive the events of his earthly sojourn reminding us, too, that he is present here and now in his glorified state.

In this volume we incorporated some of the experiences of those places which may be helpful in leading us into a prayer posture during the Lenten season: hence the emphasis on the passion and death of Jesus.

The thoughts which follow are some of the gleanings from those precious times of prayer. They are offered with the realization that it is impossible to express verbally the experiences and the sentiments of the heart. We offer them with an apology and a prayer that the Holy Spirit will empower these words to touch many hearts.

May the Holy Spirit, who "helps us in our weakness, for we do not know how to pray as we ought," grace and bless our efforts, so that our spirit may be totally in union with his Spirit. May his love, peace, and joy permeate our whole life.

ONE

Ash Wednesday:
ALMS, PRAYER, FASTING

Matthew 6:1-6, 16-18

The Mount of Beatitudes is picturesquely situated in the rolling hills of Galilee with a commanding view of the Sea of Galilee. This is one of the few uncluttered areas of Israel. It has retained much of its natural beauty, appearing as it must have been in the time of Jesus.

During the months of our spiritual renewal program, I had the privilege of going often to the Mount and resting there, in a vineyard or an olive grove, or along the seashore to be alone with the Lord.

As I tried to listen with my heart, over and above the cooing of the numerous doves and the chirping of the birds, I could almost hear the voice of Jesus loud and clear saying to the multitude, "How blest are the poor in spirit...." (Mt 5:3).

It was in this place, the Evangelists tell us, that Jesus enunciated what we call the Sermon on the Mount. Here he outlined for us the summary of his teachings. The Sermon on the Mount is often called the Magna Carta of Christianity.

The Gospel for Ash Wednesday's Liturgy of the Word is a series of extracts from that lengthy discourse. It serves as an ideal framework for our contemplations during this privileged season of Lent. They set the tone for this part of the Liturgical Cycle.

Jesus gave us some guidelines for our observance of Lent. His directives can have a powerfully transforming effect on us.

Alms. "When you give alms do not blow a horn," Jesus advises us (Mt 6:2). Sharing our material gifts is as old as the scriptures themselves. In the Old Testament, the Chosen People were to leave part of their crop for gleaning and picking by the poor. They also had a tri-annual tithe which was given to those who owned no land.

In the New Testament, Jesus teaches us the necessity of helping the poor and those in need. In the account of Judgment Day he tells us that those who have performed the works of charity will "inherit the kingdom prepared for them since the creation of the world" (Mt 25:34). He goes on to say: "I assure you, as often as you did it for one of my least brothers, you did it for me" (Mt 25:40).

Repeatedly Paul encourages generous and cheerful sharing of our gifts. John says it bluntly: "I ask you, how can God's love survive in a man who has enough of this world's goods yet closes his heart to his brother when he sees him in need" (1 Jn 3:17).

Jesus advises us not to give for purely philanthropical reasons, but with genuine disinterestedness and without ostentation. "In giving alms you are not to let your left hand know what your right hand is doing" (Mt 6:3).

Prayer. "Whenever you pray, go to your room, close the door and pray to your Father in private" (Mt 6:6).

Prayer is our relationship to our loving Father. Prayer begins with the gift of ourselves which is motivated by love. Love impels us to give. Prayer is *being for God* and letting God *be for us.*

Nothing in the gospel reveals more convincingly the absolute necessity of prayer than the example of Jesus himself. Jesus prayed always and everywhere; in seclusion, on a mountaintop, in the synagogue. His prayer was not only inspired by a desire for silent intimacy with his Father, but it was also concerned with his mission. He prayed before all the important events of his life.

Luke tells us that Jesus spent forty days in prayer before he began his public ministry. He prayed at his baptism (Lk 3:21); at the transfiguration (9:29); before teaching us the Our Father (11:1); in seclusion with his disciples (9:18); in the Garden of Gethsemani (22:41); on the cross (23:34).

Jesus' prayer was always the total gift of himself to the Father. Listen to his prayer in the Garden: "Father, if it is your will, take this cup from me: yet not my will but yours be done" (Lk 22:42).

What a lesson for us! The ideal prayer posture should be: "Here I am Lord, what is it you want?" How often the most popular prayer is "MY will be done," whereas the most perfect prayer is "YOUR will be done."

Fasting. "When you fast . . . groom your hair and wash your face" (Mt 6:17). Fasting consists in depriving ourselves of food and drink, or of some other legitimate satisfaction. Fasting occupies an important place in almost all religions. It has a strong scriptural basis.

Along with prayer and almsgiving, it is one of the essential acts which helps us express to God our humility, our hope, and our love.

Fasting moves us into a prayer posture of dependence and total abandonment to our Abba. It is a posture which helps us express our sorrow for our sinfulness.

Fasting helps us open our minds to the influence of God's grace, to his divine light. It makes us open and receptive to his will and his grace. Fasting prepares us to give ourselves totally to the Lord.

Fasting helps us to rivet our focus more directly and more permanently on God as our first priority.

Today in the Liturgy of the Word the Church would remind us of the importance of prayer, fasting, and almsgiving as we enter into this privileged season of Lent.

TWO

7

VINEYARD SONG

Isaiah 5:1-7

Israel's whole countryside is dotted with vineyards.
Some of these are spacious vineyards, others only
a small plot, still others, just a few vines around a
home. Most vineyards are planted on terraced hill-
sides facing sunward. The hot summer sun helps to
produce unusually large bunches of luscious grapes.

As we journeyed along I saw two contrasting
sights. One was a tenderly cared-for vineyard,
expertly pruned, the soil cultivated to remain
porous in order to drink in the rays of the sun as well
as the gentle rain. This vineyard was terraced so
that the sun could kiss each bunch of grapes to
sweeten and enrich the fruit as it ripened.

Not far away on my left was another vineyard,
woefully neglected and apparently abandoned. In
this vineyard the protective walls were crumbling,
the vines growing wild or being choked by weeds
and thorns. The marauding goats had stripped it of
all the most edible leaves and tender branches. At
most, I could see only a few wild, scrawny grapes.

As I sat comfortably in the shade of a large syca-
more tree with its protective branches sheltering me

from the blazing sun, I could see both vineyards before me, to the right and to the left. My thoughts turned to the Vineyard Song of Isaiah 5:1-7.

Some years ago I heard the words of this ballad, set to music. While I could not now recall the melody, the words kept running through my mind.

The prophet phrased God's disappointment in this picturesque language:

"My friend had a vineyard
on a fertile hillside
He spaded it, cleared it of stone
and planted choice vines. . . ." (Is 5:1,2).

The vineyard of the Lord is my world, the community, the environment in which I live, move, and have my being. My Father showers his gifts upon me in abundance.

Through my Baptism he has called me and planted me in his vineyard. I am "his cherished plant" (Is 5:7). As my Abba, he is sustaining me at every moment with his creating, caring, concerned love.

"He spaded it," describes how the Father has nurtured and cared for me, "his cherished plant," in his vineyard. He provided me with parents who bequeathed to me their dynamic, operative faith. He blessed me with the freedom to know, love, and worship him, in a land flowing with milk and honey.

"He. . .cleared it of stones." These stones are the obstacles and roadblocks which my sinful human nature has placed in the way of his divine life, flowing abundantly in me and flourishing within me. Each day he continues to remove the barriers which I permit to hamper his being operative within me. He does so by his forgiving, healing love. He does all this through his Son Jesus, who is my Savior and Redeemer; the One whom I meet in the Sacrament of Reconciliation.

Jesus continues to give me the gift of himself in the Eucharist. Thus he fulfills his promise: "I will not leave you orphaned" (Jn 14:18). Above all, he loves me with infinite and immutable love. "As the Father has loved me, so I have loved you. Live on in my love" (Jn 15:9).

He has been lavishly generous with me, his cherished plant. He has given me not only life, but also health of body, mind, and spirit. He has surrounded me with family and friends. He has enriched me with gifts of food, drink, sleep; moments of happiness; sight, hearing, speech.

As these myriad gifts crowded in my mind, the heart-rending question of the Father kept haunting me: "What more was there to do for my vineyard that I had not done?" (Is 5:4).

Even though the question may seem to be a rhetorical one, I felt it was addressed to me personally, at that moment. I felt that the Father was waiting for my answer. What more could I have done for you, my cherished plant, that I have not yet done?

Lent is an ideal time to ask ourselves, What kind of grapes are we producing? Lent is a time for pruning. As we bask in the sunshine of God's loving presence, we can more easily recognize the thorns and briars which clutter our lives. He assures us that he will help us to remove them if we are open and receptive to his presence and love.

Like porous soil, our hearts must remain ever ready to receive the gentle rain of his divine life. Let us pray always for the grace to detach ourselves from the plastic, neon gods which so easily clutter the vineyard of the Lord, and which cause us to produce only "wild grapes" (Is 5:2).

THREE

FLIGHT INTO EGYPT

Matthew 2:13-18

At the very beginning of his earthly existence
Jesus was rejected. Soon after his birth, an
angel appeared to Joseph and said: "Get up, take
the child and his mother and flee to Egypt.…
Herod is searching for the child to destroy him" (Mt
2:13).

Herod is the quintessence of all that is opposed to
the kingdom of God. His pride and ambition blinded him to the real import of the Wise Men's visit. He
missed the message completely. His inordinate desire for power, prestige, and possessions created
within him a dreadful fear of any rival. Maddened
by this fear, he spread death and destruction.

The route which the Holy Family must have
taken into Egypt was much the same as the road to
Gaza today. Gaza is in the southwesterly part of
what is now Israel. It is very close to the Egyptian
border.

Our journey to Gaza was along the same route
over which Joseph must have led Mary and Jesus.
Along the highway today there are numerous mili-
tary checkpoints. Everyone traveling that route

today is suspect, frequently searched, and made to feel unwelcome and unwanted. It was a powerful reminder of the suspicion, mistrust, fear, and tension which prevailed in the court of Herod, at the time of Jesus.

Gaza is densely populated with displaced persons, driven from their homes, deprived of human dignity, living in dire poverty, with only the bare essentials for human sustenance. They are suspected and unwanted. Their only crime is to have been born at this time, in this place, and of a certain ethnic background.

I could not help but think that it was the same crime of which Jesus was guilty. He came into a world to bring Good News, but that world rejected him already when he was a helpless Babe. How pathetically John reminds us: "To his own he came, yet his own did not accept him" (Jn 1:11).

In the Milk Grotto in Bethlehem there is a shrine depicting the Holy Family on their flight into Egypt. I have never before seen such life-like statues. Mary is riding on a donkey, tenderly holding the Child Jesus, who is peacefully sleeping with a little smile on his face. Mary's expression is one of quiet, peaceful joy. One would hardly suspect that they are in flight for their very lives.

Joseph is shown with a staff in one hand, and leading the donkey with the other. He is tenderly and lovingly looking back at Mary and Jesus. Never before have I seen such an expression on a statue. Joseph's eyes are sparkling with peace, joy, and love. While his eyes seem to be dancing, his smile reveals a heart filled with confidence, trust, dedication, and devotion to duty. Even though it is a statue, his expression is alive, human, other-worldly.

This shrine in the Milk Grotto spoke to me about the flight into Egypt. The expression of joy, happiness and peace on Joseph's face touched me deeply.

Even though the Holy Family was being driven out by hatred, jealousy, and murderous intent, they still proceeded with confidence and trust. Joseph knew, even though he did not understand, that somehow, this was God's will. He also knew that God would protect them and provide for them in a foreign land. Mary, Joseph, and the Infant all rested in the security of God's love as they journeyed across the burning sands.

What confidence and reassurance this event of salvation history can bring to us! "Is it possible that he who did not spare his own Son but handed him over for the sake of us all will not grant us all things besides?" (Rom 8:32).

If we are going to follow Jesus so closely as to be his disciples, if we are going to be identified with him, then we too will suffer persecution. Jesus himself prepared us for the misunderstandings, the insults, and the ridicule which we can expect if we are to be his followers.

"If you find that the world hates you, know that it has hated me before you. If you belonged to the world, it would love you as its own; the reason it hates you is that you do not belong to the world. But I chose you out of the world. They will harry you as they harried me. They will respect your words as much as they respected mine" (Jn 15:18-20).

Jesus not only prepared us for the attitude of the world, but he prayed for us in his highpriestly prayer at the Last Supper:

"For these I pray, not for the world, but for these
you have given me. . .

"they are really yours. . .

"protect them with your holy name. . . .

"I gave them your word, and the world hated
them for it. . . .

"I do not ask you to take them out of the world,
but to guard them from the evil one. . . ." (Jn 17:9-19).

FOUR

NAZARETH'S REJECTION

Luke 4:14-30

In Nazareth, recent soundings and excavations have uncovered the "brow of the hill" over which the people of the town intended to hurl Jesus when they expelled him from the synagogue. For many years the brow of the hill was pointed out as being far removed from the heart of Nazareth. This recently discovered "brow of the hill" is close to the modern, new and large Basilica dedicated by Pope Paul VI in 1964. It is also close to the spot where the synagogue of Nazareth once stood.

A small, ancient synagogue stands there, now, near the brow of the hill. It is, like all the other buildings, made of cut stone. It is very simple, spartan and unadorned.

As we visited the synagogue and seated ourselves on the stone bench which is a ledge along the wall, I had the privilege of reading aloud Luke's account of Jesus at Nazareth. After the reading we spent time in silence, contemplating the implications of all that happened here.

We listened to Jesus reading the words of the Prophet Isaiah:

"The Spirit of the Lord is upon me
    therefore he has anointed me.
He has sent me to bring glad tidings to
    the poor
    to proclaim liberty to captives,
to announce a year of favor from the Lord"
    (Is 61:1f).

I could almost hear Jesus say audibly, "Today this scripture passage is fulfilled in your hearing" (Lk 4:21).

The response of the people of his day moved from one stage to another. At first, "they marveled at the appealing discourse which came from his lips" (Lk 4:22). Matthew says, "They were filled with amazement" (Mt 13:54).

Another reaction began to take shape. Doubt began to cloud their minds: "Is not this Joseph's son?" (Lk 4:22).

Fear and doubt soon turned to rejection. We are so apt to reject what we do not understand. "The whole audience in the synagogue was filled with indignation" (Lk 4:28).

Fear often turns into violence. "They rose up and expelled him from the town, leading him to the brow of the hill on which it was built and intending to hurl him over the edge" (Lk 4:29f)

While Jesus was willing to accept persecution and misunderstanding, nevertheless, his hour had not yet come according to the Father's plan. Hence, he proved even more conclusively the power of his words when he "went straight through their midst and walked away" (Lk 4:30).

As I sat there in the warmth of the early spring, I reflected on my own personal reactions to Jesus. How much I am like the seed in the parable (Mt 13:4-23). In the soil of my heart I find the well-trodden, hardened path, the rocky ground, the thorn-covered terrain.

My first reaction to the inspiration of God's grace is often enthusiasm and amazement. I am eager and anxious to respond graciously and generously to Jesus.

But, then, how quickly I begin to have misgivings, fears. Is Jesus asking too much? I fear to discover his will more clearly, lest he ask for more than I am prepared to give. I begin to doubt whether it was the voice of Jesus speaking, at all. I rationalize, and disuade myself.

Soon I feel rejection welling up within me. Since the will of Jesus crosses my will, I cannot possibly accept it. How often my prayer is, "Let my will be done," instead of, "your will be done."

The next step in my rebellion is hostility, even though it may be only momentary. Often when a deep disappointment, severe suffering, or a heavy cross comes my way, I have feelings of anger or bitterness toward my loving Father.

Jesus "went straight through their midst and walked away" (Lk 4:30). Seemingly, he walks out of my life and lets me fend for myself, until I realize not only my complete dependence upon him, but also how very much he loves me: "As the Father has loved me, so I have loved you" (Jn 15:9).

As Jesus went straight through the crowd and walked away, let us walk with him.

FIVE

JESUS IS TEMPTED

Matthew 4:1-11

Jericho is probably the first walled city in the world, and it dates back some 10,000 years. From the ancient city of Jericho you get a good view of the Mount of Temptation.

It looks like a high, bleak, barren mountain of rock. There is no vegetation on the mountain. On the eastern wall of the mountain clings a Greek Orthodox monastery. This is built in front of the grotto where, according to tradition, Jesus fasted and was tempted. The monastery retains its contemplative atmosphere because it is not easily accessible.

The summit of the mountain is flat. A wall encloses a chapel which marks the site of the place where "the devil took him up into a very high mountain."

After his baptism in the River Jordan by John the Baptist, "Jesus was led into the desert by the Spirit to be tempted by the devil." Jesus went into the desert to fast and pray before he began his public ministry.

In times of prayer and fasting a soul is very vulnerable to the onslaught of the evil one. Jesus was no exception. The devil used every ruse to wean

Jesus away from doing the will of the Father in beginning his teaching mission.

The temptations which Jesus faced were the sum-total of all the temptations which the Israelites endured in the desert. They succumbed to these temptations and turned away from God. However, Jesus succeeded in overcoming each one of these temptations and victoriously routed the devil.

These temptations which beset Jesus are the same temptations which face us on our pilgrimage back to the Father.

In essence the temptations were subtle. The devil was not trying to openly thwart the mission of Jesus, but was suggesting that the Father's plan was impractical. The devil was trying to persuade Jesus to do it the easy way: Be sensational and you will attract followers in droves.

The tactics of the evil one are still the same in our lives. He is very subtle, but not too powerful if we stay close to Jesus.

Lent is a time when we are striving to deepen our personal relationship with Jesus. Prayer enriches that relationship. Fasting is an ideal prayer posture. Be assured that we will be faced with many temptations during this time as we strive for our goal.

Jesus showed us the way to counteract these temptations. The devil quoted scripture to distract Jesus from doing the Father's will. Jesus reversed the procedure and quoted the words of sacred scripture back to the devil, to assure him that he was doing everything according to the Word of God. He used the words of scripture to give his Father praise and glory.

When we are tempted and when it is obvious that

the allurements are really coming from the evil one, we can act against him in the same way.

When we are tempted we can use the power of exorcism which we received by virtue of our Baptism. A simple formula is: "In the name of Jesus, I drive you out." We always call upon the name and power of Jesus.

The second weapon is the same as one Jesus used: we can use what the devil intended to lead us away from God to praise and thank our Father.

Here is a little example. Suppose that we were going to spend an hour in prayer. Our place of prayer was very quiet and undisturbed, but, as we enter into prayer, a lot of noise and racket is being raised by some workmen in the vicinity. Our first impulse would be to become disgruntled and angry. Then we discern that this is a temptation. Immediately we can exorcise the evil one and then begin to thank and praise God for our gift of hearing. We remember that we have heard so many wonderful things in our lifetime: good music, the birds singing, our friends and family speaking to us.

With Jesus we can say: "Away with you, Satan!" and with Jesus we can say: "Father, Lord of heaven and earth, to you I offer praise; for what you have revealed to the merest children" (Mt. 11:25).

SIX

OUR FATHER

Matthew 6: 7-15

Mount Olivet was one of Jesus' favorite places for prayer. He often went to this sacred hill. There, in the seclusion of a cave or under the arms of an olive tree, he prayed in the stillness of the night, away from the hostility and harassment of the City. The evangelists speak of his prayer as "spending the night in communion with God" (Lk 6:12), or "there he was absorbed in prayer" (Mk 1:35).

Today the tall slender steeple of the Pater Noster Church on the top of the Mount of Olives can be seen from great distances. This is generally accepted as the place where Jesus taught the disciples the Lord's Prayer. Luke writes: "One day he was praying in a certain place. When he had finished one of his disciples asked him: 'Lord, teach us to pray'. . ." (Lk 11:1).

Today as you enter the courtyard of the Pater Noster Shrine, you proceed down an arched veranda. Arranged on the wall side of the veranda you will pass forty-one large plaques, each with the Pater Noster written on it in a different language.

Under the half-built walls of an unfinished church, a walk leads into a cavernous grotto where Jesus supposedly sought shelter and solitude with his disciples. It was in this little sanctuary that Jesus responded to their request when they asked him, "Lord, teach us to pray" (Lk 11:1).

Fortunately, this grotto has been left in its natural state. I found a comfortable place to sit with a large rock as a back rest, many thoughts crowding into my mind as I began to reflect on this prayer coming from the lips of Jesus.

Jesus taught us some tremendous truths in this prayer. Note that the first three petitions are directed toward God. The Our Father is concerned with the glory of God.

When we call God our Father, all other things fall into their proper relationship. In the first place, we establish the right relationship with our fellow men. If God is our Father and we are his adopted sons and daughters, then we are brothers and sisters to one another.

When we recognize God as our loving Abba, we also relate to ourselves properly. There are moments when it is hard for us to accept ourselves as we are. We really do not love ourselves. However, when we recognize that God is our Father we know that we are loved and lovable. It is crucial for us to recognize this.

Thirdly, these petitions help us to establish a right relationship to God. God is the transcendent God of heaven and earth. He is always approachable as our Father. He, as Father, is always concerned about every detail of our life.

The second part of the Lord's Prayer deals with our own needs. It is concerned with our essential needs and the three spheres of time in which we move.

First, we ask God for 'bread'; that is, for all the things which are necessary for the maintenance of life, both physical and spiritual. Thus, we bring our present need to our Father, who wants to be a generous God.

Secondly, we ask for the forgiveness of all our faults and failures, our unfaithfulness and sinfulness. In this prayer we bring the past before our Father.

Thirdly, we ask not to be subjected to trial, but to be delivered from all evil. Here we are committing the future to God's loving care.

When we ask for our daily bread, we direct our thoughts to God our Father, relying on his providential and caring love for each one of his children. When we recognize our sinfulness and turn to God for healing and forgiveness, we immediately come to Jesus — our Savior and Redeemer. When we are aware of the future help we will need in time of temptation and trial, our thoughts go to the Holy Spirit. He is the Comforter, Strengthener, and Illuminator, the One who remains with us and within us.

All too soon the time came for me to leave this hallowed spot. Before departing I besought the disciples to pray with me as I begged, "Lord, teach me to pray."

SEVEN

First Station:
JESUS SENTENCED

John 19:1-16

Jesus was brought bound by his captors to the Pretorium where the governor resided. He was delivered over to Pilate so that he might ratify the sentence of death which the Sanhedrin had already pronounced.

Pilate examined Jesus privately in the palace, which is now the Omariyeh College. This is the starting point of the way of the cross today. The public part of the trial was held in the big courtyard, called in Greek the Lithostrotos, or Stone Pavement. The Franciscan Fathers care for the Chapel of Condemnation which marks this spot, while the Lithostrotos, which joins the chapel, is in the lower level of the Convent of the Sisters of Sion.

It was on this Stone Pavement, called Gabbatha in Hebrew, that Pilate argued in vain with the chief priests and the temple guards. His vacillation ended when the accusers shouted: "If you free this man you are no friend of Caesar" (Jn 19:12). John records the pathetic outcome of that trial in one brief statement: "In the end Pilate handed Jesus

28

over to be crucified" (Jn 19:16).

As Jesus stood before that clamoring mob, the words of the Prophet Jeremiah were fulfilled. "Yet I, like a trusting lamb led to slaughter, had not realized that they were hatching plots against me: 'Let us destroy the tree in its vigor; let us cut him off from the land of the living, so that his name will be spoken no more'" (Jer 11:19).

In the face of the false accusations and the clamoring for his blood, Jesus remained silent. His silence spoke many things.

In the first place, the charges were so groundless and so falsified that a defense was useless. His silence was far more eloquent than any verbal defense.

Peter, the first pope, reminds us: "He did no wrong; no deceit was found in his mouth. When he was insulted, he returned no insult. When he was made to suffer, he did not counter with threats. Instead, he delivered himself up to the One who judges justly" (1 Pt 2:22-23).

Jesus was now showing us by way of example what he had taught about the way of life which he came to introduce to his followers. In his Sermon on the Mount Jesus said: "Offer no resistance to injury. When a person strikes you on the right cheek, turn and offer him the other" (Mt 5:39).

Isaiah had predicted this kind of treatment for the Servant of the Lord: "A grave was assigned him among the wicked and a burial place with evil-doers, though he had done no wrong, nor spoken any falsehood" (Is 53:9).

Secondly, Jesus remained silent because in a certain sense he was guilty of all of which he was accused. He had taken upon himself the weight of our sinfulness. Again St. Peter says: "In his own body he brought your sins to the cross, so that all of us, dead to sin, could live in accord with God's will. By his wounds you were healed" (1 Pt 2:24).

John, the beloved disciple, expresses this truth so powerfully: "Love, then, consists in this: not that we have loved God, but that he has loved us and has sent his Son as an offering for our sins" (1 Jn 4:10). In the same Letter, John also says: "He is an offering for our sins, and not for our sins only, but for those of the whole world" (1 Jn 2:2).

Some spiritual writers see Jesus in the younger brother in the parable of the Prodigal Son. Jesus having taken upon himself the burden of our sins returns to his Father who receives him most graciously and compassionately. They see in the elder brother the righteous who point an accusing finger at Jesus and at all whom they judge to be sinners.

Since Jesus accepted this death penalty silently for us, John advises us about our own attitude and mode of conduct. He says: "The way we come to understand love was that he laid down his life for us; we too must lay down our lives for our brothers" (1 Jn 3:16).

That injunction is no small order. In fact, it would sound ridiculous unless Jesus himself stood before Pilate and heard him say: "Take him and crucify him yourselves; I find no case against him" (Jn 19:16).

EIGHT

Second Station
JESUS RECEIVES HIS CROSS

Philippians 2:6-11

When I was making the way of the cross privately, I went into the Convent of the Sisters of Sion for the time of contemplation on the second station. In the lower level of the Convent is the Lithostrotos, the stone pavement of Pilate's courtyard, with its huge flagstones still intact.

It is a deeply moving experience to walk across this pavement, remembering the scenes enacted here on the first Good Friday. On the wall is a large colorful mosaic of Jesus accepting the cross. Jesus is depicted all alone facing you, with the cross slightly off to his side. The cross is resting lightly upon his left shoulder while his right hand is resting on the upright beam.

This portrayal appeals to me because it conveys Jesus' willingness to accept the instrument of his death. In fact there is a calm and peaceful expression on his face. Even though it meant his death, Jesus must have welcomed the cross, for he was fulfilling the will of his Father by "obediently accepting even death, death on a cross" (Phil 2:8).

Since the day on which Jesus accepted his cross on the Stone Pavement, the cross has become the symbol of the followers of Christ. It is the standard of our Christian way of life. In fact Jesus made the cross the condition for becoming one of his followers. He said without equivocation: "Whoever wishes to be my follower must deny his very self, take up his cross each day, and follow in my steps" (Lk 9:23). There is no other option.

As Jesus accepted his cross he was manifesting his total dependence on his Father with all trust and confidence. This is genuine poverty of spirit.

In accepting his cross Jesus was teaching us some valuable lessons about poverty of spirit. Jesus freely chose man's poverty as a part of his human condition, his reality. Jesus came to love man on man's level; therefore he accepted his poor condition. Man's poverty is sickness, the infirmities of old age, his inability to understand, and all his other physical, spiritual, and psychological limitations.

Jesus met man on his level. He came as a helpless Babe to be at the mercy of others. He was a poor man working with other men to earn a livelihood. The sweat of hard labor prepared him for his bloody sweat in the Garden. He accepted no honor, no temporal power. He chose mildness, not violence, not force but love. With real poverty he received his cross.

We can come close to Jesus more easily because he is poor. He is more approachable in his poverty than in his omnipotence. His poverty speaks more plainly than his omniscience. His poverty is nearer to us than his majestic beauty. Because of his poverty, Jesus stays with us to listen to us, to comfort us when we weep, to console us in loneliness, to heal us when we hurt.

In his poverty Jesus accepted creation which was made perfect by his Father, but had been corrupted by man's sin. He began here with his cross, to free us and creation "to share in the glorious freedom of the children of God" (Rom 8:18-25).

We manifest our poverty by accepting our own cross. At first, our human nature rebels against the cross. We groan inwardly, and bitterly complain about its weight and its size. At times we may openly and violently rebel against the cross. Then, gradually and almost ashamedly, we recognize that we are not carrying our cross alone. Jesus reminded us "Apart from me you can do nothing" (Jn 15:5). With him, we can do all things.

Jesus is our Simon of Cyrene. He shoulders our cross and bids us to follow in his footsteps. He not only encourages us with the words: "My grace is enough for you," but he guarantees us that "in weakness, power will reach perfection" (2 Cor 12:9).

As I sat in the convent, on a hard bench without a back, I was tempted to stand up to leave. Before I did so I took a long loving look at the large mosaic of Jesus accepting his cross. He gifted me graciously, for it was another hour before I left. Then, as I prepared to leave, my heart whispered: "Thank you, Jesus, for loving me enough to accept that cruel cross for me."

NINE

Third Station
JESUS FALLS THE FIRST TIME

Matthew 11:28-30

As a devout pilgrim prays with Jesus along the Via Dolorosa, he will come to a corner in the El Wad Road which marks the spot where Jesus fell the first time under the cross. There is a little chapel here donated by the Polish people. Over the portal leading into the chapel is a high-relief depicting this first fall of Jesus. It is a very narrow chapel, but it serves well to commemorate this first fall of Jesus. This scene of Jesus' fall is likewise depicted over the small altar.

When I arrived, the chapel was practically deserted. Only a few people were there. Soon they left to continue their own devotional way of the cross. Again I had the privilege of being alone with the Lord in this moment of his sorrowful journey to Calvary.

In spite of our traditional way of picturing Jesus carrying his whole cross, there seems to have been a common custom at this time to place only the heavy crossbeam over the shoulders of the victim and then tie his arms securely to the beam. This rendered him helpless, with no means of escaping. In this helpless position, the prisoner was forced to walk to the place of execution where the upright portion of the cross was already in position.

If this is the way Jesus was bound to the crossbeam, we can imagine his helplessness as he staggered along. Furthermore, he would not be able to break his fall, or to help himself rise after a painful fall. Thus Jesus suffered excruciating pain because of this fall. He experienced much more pain as the soldiers pulled and jerked him to his feet.

As I pondered this first fall of Jesus, I thought of my many falls when my own cross seemed to be heavy or even unbearable.

Life has its share of disappointments, worries, and anxieties. There are moments of little persecutions, when we are misunderstood, criticized, or have even our best efforts and intentions misinterpreted. There are times when in God's mysterious plan, we are asked to accept some physical suffering, be it some transitory pain, or a lingering illness. These too can be a portion of the cross which life holds out to us.

Jesus understood the burdens which we would experience. He is prepared to help us shoulder each day's cross and follow in his footsteps. He is also on hand to help us rise after our own fall beneath the cross.

Jesus invites us to come to him in times of crisis. Listen to his invitation: "Come to me, all you who are weary and find life burdensome, and I will refresh you" (Mt 11:28). Jesus can refresh us because he experienced the burden of these crosses.

He knows that our falls may be unrighteous reactions — anger toward someone, defensiveness, or self-pity.

Jesus reminds us that we are not alone, but that he is always with us. He invites us to: "Take my yoke upon your shoulders." Jesus assures us it is his yoke he is asking us to share.

A yoke is a harness used by oxen or donkeys, enabling them to pull a heavy load. Usually a pair or team of animals are harnessed together. Jesus reminds us it is his yoke. He is pulling the greater portion of the load. We are asked only to help him.

Our falls will be less frequent if we learn from him. He bids us: "Learn from me for I am gentle and humble of heart." As we spend time in prayer, our hearts are transformed. We do become more gentle and humble of heart, even though we may not be consciously aware of it.

This transformation will change our attitude. When our focus is on the fallen Jesus, our own burdens will be minimized. The acuteness of our pain will gradually disappear.

As we gaze at Jesus stumbling and falling beneath that heavy load, and as we are willing to put our heads into his yoke, we will hear his encouraging words: "Your souls will find rest, for my yoke is easy and my burden light."

TEN

Fourth Station
JESUS MEETS HIS MOTHER

Luke 2:41-52

A long the Via Dolorosa you can step off the narrow, noisy street into a small rectangular oratory which commemorates the meeting of Jesus and his Mother as he carried his cross to Calvary. This small chapel is very near the entrance of the Church of Our Lady of the Spasm.

The Fourth Station is depicted in bas-relief marble over the altar in this tiny chapel. With reverence and devotion we recall this meeting as another one of the swords which Simeon predicted would pierce the heart of Mary.

Mary risked the scorn and ridicule of the enemies of Jesus. She even risked physical danger as she approached her Son. Nothing would prevent her from being with Jesus in this "his hour."

We do not know whether Mary was able to speak a few words of comfort and love to her Son. We do know, however, that her presence must have brought great consolation to Jesus. Perhaps they were only able to look at each other. What love must have been expressed in Mary's pained counte-

nance! Her look at Jesus told him how much she
loved him, how much she wanted to wipe the dirt
and spittle from his sacred face, how much she
wanted to help him carry his cross.

In turn, when Jesus looked at Mary, what a message of love that look must have communicated!
Jesus wanted his Mother to know how much he
loved her, how much he appreciated her presence
and comfort and consolation.

Mary had many times experienced the piercing
pain of the rejection of her son, and also the
stabbing pain of her separation from him. When
the angel of the Lord said to Joseph "Get up, take
the child and his mother and flee to Egypt" (Mt
2:13), Mary suffered from the rejection which was
already confronting her Infant Son.

Mary also experienced the pain of separation
when Jesus was lost in the Temple when he was
twelve years old.

When Jesus left his home in Nazareth to journey
to the Jordan to begin his public ministry, Mary
again knew the piercing sword which Simeon predicted. Even during his public life, when his
Mother and brethren sought him out, they knew
that his primary priority was the will of the Father.
The will of the Father meant his total absorption in
bringing the Good News to all men.

All these separations caused Mary much suffering, but this encounter along the Via Dolorosa was
even more painful, because it carried with it such
finality.

Mary is still fulfilling her role as Mother today.
Jesus established the Church as his Body, which is

continuing the mystery of salvation here on earth.

We are the Church and we are members of Christ's body. We are the Church on pilgrimage back to the Father. Our pilgrimage is often a way of the cross. We are not travelling that Via Dolorosa alone. From the Cross Jesus gave us his Mother to be with us, to accompany us.

The Second Vatican Council once again declared that Mary's role was to be the Mother of the Church, and our Mother. As our Mother, she is journeying along with us. She is there to comfort and console us when our cross seems unbearable. She meets us to reassure us of the great love which Jesus has for us, and also to guarantee her own undying love for us, her children.

As we meet her, we are reminded of Cana and the power of her intercession. Let us ask her to implore her Son to change the water of our mediocrity, the water of our fears, the water of our rebellion into the sparkling wine of love, spurring us on to take up our cross daily and follow him.

ELEVEN

Fifth Station
SIMON OF CYRENE HELPS JESUS

Mark 15:21

The three synoptic Gospels record the fact that a certain Simon of Cyrene was conscripted and forced to help Jesus carry his cross. Today the place where this event of salvation history took place is indicated at a point where the Via Dolorosa begins to ascend steeply toward Golgotha. A small Franciscan oratory stands at the spot.

I was fortunate enough to be at the oratory when no one else was present. Even though the street noises were as loud as usual, the hallowed seclusion of the little chapel led me into contemplating this theme and what it means in my life. The chapel is adorned with a statue depicting Simon being conscripted to help Jesus carry his cross.

In the time of Jesus, Palestine was occupied by the Romans. They had a law which empowered them to force any man into service for any task at any given moment. The sign of this conscription was a tap on the shoulder by a Roman soldier with the blunt side of his spearhead.

In prayer we can speculate what took place here.

Simon was from Cyrene in Africa. Perhaps he had come to Jerusalem to celebrate the Passover. He might have been curious about the noise and confusion which he heard in the street, and moved in that direction to observe more closely what was happening.

According to the custom of that day, when a criminal was condemned to death, a cross was prepared and laid upon his shoulders. The group was then ready to move to the place of execution outside the city. The normal procedure required five soldiers. Four of them formed an open square around the prisoner, while the fifth soldier walked in front carrying a board for everyone to see. On this board was written the crime of which the criminal was convicted. This cordon often took the longest route to the place of execution so that as many people as possible could see the sign which would hopefully deter them from committing any crime, especially any uprising against the Roman government.

As I lingered in this little oratory, I could well imagine that at first Simon must have bitterly resented being pressed into this kind of service. He wanted no part of any execution. No doubt, he hated the Roman soldiers as well as the criminal whose cross he was forced to carry. He might have thought, not too kindly, that if this Jesus had been a model citizen, he, Simon would not have fallen heir to this degrading service.

We can also speculate that Simon intended to reach the spot of execution and then rush off as quickly as possible. Yet in spite of these feelings, something about Jesus fascinated him. Jesus' silent response to the insults and derision hurled at him amazed Simon. Furthermore, there were many in the crowd who seemed to reverence and respect him. More and more Simon must have felt drawn to Jesus without knowing the reason.

There is a possibility that Simon did eventually become one of Jesus' disciples. Paul mentions a Rufus in his Letter to the Romans (16:13). Recall that Mark says Simon was "the father of Alexander and Rufus" (Mk 15:31). Luke also mentions a "Symeon known as Niger" in the Acts (13:1). "Niger" was a common appellation of a person who had come from Africa and Simon was from Cyrene in Africa. This is only speculation, but it may be conducive to our prayer.

In our daily apostolate, Jesus is inviting us to a deeper, more committed discipleship. In the first place, he asks us to take up our own cross daily. In fact, Jesus makes that a condition of our discipleship. He says to us: "Whoever wishes to be my follower must deny his very self, take us his cross each day, and follow in my steps" (Lk 9:23). Sometime later he repeats these conditions without equivocation: "Anyone who does not take up his cross and follow me cannot be my disciple" (Lk 14:27).

Jesus also invites us to share in helping him carry his cross. His cross is the cross which his Body is carrying today. Since we are members of his Body, it is our cross too. We can enjoy the same privilege which Simon had even though it may seem paradoxical. Like Simon we, too, may cringe or even rebel at the weight of the cross or the humiliation which it may bring. There is one compelling factor which drives us to accept that cross, and that is love.

At first Simon must have rebelled when he was forced to assist Jesus. Gradually love reached out to him and he gladly shouldered more and more of the weight of the cross.

Once we have experienced Jesus' love for us — a love so great that he willingly and freely accepted his own cross for us — then we cannot help but become a disciple who takes up his cross daily and follows in the steps of the Master.

TWELVE

Sixth Station
VERONICA

Matthew 10:28-33

For several reasons the shrine of the Sixth Station is my favorite place along the Way of the Cross. It may not be the most important, nor is it authenticated in scripture, but, for me, it is the most devotional. I have always found this spot conducive to prayer.

The Sixth Station along the Via Dolorosa is marked by a grotto-like chapel built out of cut stone. You enter this oratory from the street level, stepping down a few stairs into the chapel. The chapel is very spartan in its simplicity. The bare walls and vaulted ceiling are stone. The furnishings are few. The altar is a huge slab of stone about twelve inches thick which has been made table-smooth on top, and is roughly hewn on the sides. It is supported by a single pillar cut from a huge rock.

Behind the altar is a picture of the face of Jesus, apparently the imprint of his sacred countenance left on Veronica's cloth. A seven-branched candelabrum stands behind the altar below the picture. The only other furnishing is a thin, free-standing iron crucifix placed to the right of the altar.

The only provision for the worshipper is a stone ledge which serves as a bench along the wall, nothing else.

There is a real atmosphere of prayer about this chapel. One of the reasons, I am sure, is the fact that this oratory is found in the convent of the Little Sisters of Jesus who were founded according to the Rule of Brother Charles of Jesus. These Sisters live here and care for the shrine. They are contemplatives living in the world. They speak seldom, but smile frequently. Even though the noises of the passersby on the narrow street can be heard, the chapel still has a prayerful atmosphere about it. I am sure that the presence and the prayers of the Little Sisters contribute much to this hallowed atmosphere.

According to tradition, as Jesus was carrying his cross on the way to Calvary, he passed the home of Veronica. According to the same tradition, Veronica saw the pitiable condition of Jesus. Blood was trickling down from his crowned head obscuring his vision, his sacred face was covered with blood, dirt, and spittle. Veronica courageously elbowed her way through the crowd of his enemies, broke through the protective guard of soldiers, and presented Jesus with a cloth with which to wipe his face and obtain, at least, some momentary relief. Jesus was most pleased with this courageous act of love. As usual, Jesus was always thinking of others. When he returned the cloth to her, his sacred face had been imprinted upon it.

The holy woman, whom we call Veronica, was a

woman of courage. She braved physical harm as she forced her way up to Jesus. She probably encountered the ridicule of his enemies, yet she was not daunted. Her love impelled her to minister to Jesus, regardless of the price she might have to pay.

This act of kindness was also a public profession of her faith in Jesus. Veronica believed in Jesus with that kind of faith, of commitment. It is certainly not popular to openly declare faith in a person or a cause which is being annihilated and going down in utter defeat. Veronica believed, and that faith prompted her into action.

Veronica could not have had that deep faith, nor the courage of her conviction, unless she loved. She had come to love Jesus. Love knows no bounds.

As I lingered in this haven of peace, I reviewed my own life. Would I be sufficiently courageous to manifest my faith and my love to the extent that Veronica did?

Jesus is suffering in his Body all around us each day. His Body, the people of God — especially the poor, the handicapped, the underprivileged — are suffering as they struggle along their own way of the cross.

Jesus is looking for champions who will present the towel of empathy, love, and compassion to them — nay, to him, for he said: "I assure you, as often as you did it for one of my least brothers, you did it for me" (Mt 25:40).

The name "Veronica" means true image. Veronica certainly was the true image of the love, compassion, and kindness which radiates from the heart of Jesus. I am sure Jesus was thinking about all the

Veronicas when he said: "Whoever acknowledges me before men I will acknowledge before my Father in heaven" (Mt 10:32).

Ask Veronica to intercede for you that you may become a "True Image."

THIRTEEN

Seventh Station
SECOND FALL

Romans 7:13-25

As a person progresses along the Via Dolorosa he or she will come to the Seventh Station which recalls the painful second fall of Jesus. One finds here a little chapel under the devoted care of the Franciscans. This chapel houses a great Roman column.

According to tradition, there was a city gate here in the old wall of Jerusalem. It was here that Jesus fell helplessly to the ground. Tradition also informs us that the notice of the cause for which Jesus was being executed was posted here. This site has often been called Judgment Gate.

This second fall speaks volumes to us. As we ponder this scene today with the risen Jesus, he would remind us of the dreadful physical pain which this fall caused him. With his arms tied to the crossbeam, there was no way by which he could cushion his fall onto the hard, dirty pavement. Once more he experienced the pain of rejection. His enemies feared that he would not reach the place of execution, thus depriving them of the malicious delight they were anticipating. At the crescendo of

48

insults being hurled at him, the piercing sword of rejection penetrated more deeply into his Sacred Heart.

As Jesus staggered along, the enormity of sin, the malice of the human heart, the utter rejection of his love, must have startled him, momentarily causing him to crumble under its weight.

Unknown to his enemies, Jesus had no intention of lying here to pour out his life's blood. He came to rescue us from our sins. He loves us with an infinite love, and love can never be satisfied until it has given all.

How aptly the prophet describes him as the Suffering Servant:

> Yet it was our infirmities that he bore,
>   our sufferings that he endured...
> We had all gone astray like sheep,
>   each following his own way;
> But the Lord laid upon him
>   the guilt of us all... (Isaiah 53: 4, 6)

Jesus reminds us over and over again in the Good News that he has come to free us from the bonds of sin. He has come as our Redeemer, our Savior. Sin is saying no to love. Sin is a refusal to love. Jesus said very explicitly: "He who obeys the commandments he has from me is the man who loves me" (Jn 14:21).

As I pondered this second fall of Jesus, I thought of the countless times I preferred my own will to his! How often I neglected to reach out in love! How often I have resolved to change my life, only to fall back into my old sinful ways!

In his Letter to the Romans, Paul shares some re-
flections on sin and death. Paul yearns to fulfill
God's will perfectly in his life, but fails so frequently. He says: "the desire to do right is there but
not the power." Yet Paul does not lose hope, for he
knows that Jesus will come to his rescue. Listen to
his words: "What a wretched man I am! Who can
free me from this body under the power of death?"
Then he recognizes that his only hope is in Jesus and
he exclaims: "All praise to God, through Jesus
Christ our Lord!" (Rom 7:13-24).

Our hope too rests in the great love which Jesus
has for us. It was this love which impelled him to
rise after this fall and continue his tortuous way to
Calvary.

As I lingered here with the din of human traffic
all around me, I thought of the many rejections
which Jesus is receiving even today. How many
passersby hurried by this station without the
slightest thought of what took place here. How
many do not even know Jesus as their Lord and
Savior!

How many people throughout the world are
totally oblivious of the love which wrought our salvation! How many are too busy, too preoccupied
with mundane interests, to be concerned about the
God who loves them! How painful must their indif-
ference be to Jesus!

Amid the hubbub I prayed that I might become
more and more conscious of his love for me, because
I recognized myself in those who forget him.

Before I moved along to the next station I asked
to be so gifted that I may reflect his love to others.

FOURTEEN.

Eighth Station
JESUS COMFORTS
THE WEEPING WOMEN

Luke 23: 27-31

If you were walking along the Via Dolorosa in the Old City of Jerusalem, you might very easily miss the Eighth Station where Jesus met the weeping women. It is marked only by a brief inscription incised into one of the many stones making up the wall of a building.

Here Jesus met a group of women who were mourning over his sorrowful condition. According to the Talmud, the aristocratic women of Jerusalem used to prepare a heavily drugged drink to dull the pain of a condemned criminal. These women may have offered this drink to Jesus. Apparently Jesus did not accept the drink they offered, even though he was grateful for their kindness. In this dreadful hour of his suffering, Jesus was not seeking comfort for himself, but rather was reaching out to comfort others.

In the Garden of Gethsemani Jesus manifested his loving concern for others. When Simon Peter severed the ear of Malchus, the highpriest's slave,

Jesus "touched the ear and healed the man" (Lk 22:51). Likewise, he was not thinking about himself, but pleaded for the safety of his disciples when he said in the Garden: "If I am the one you want, let these men go" (Jn 18:8).

Along the Way of the Cross, Jesus was sensitive to the suffering of the women. This is characteristic of his loving concern for others. He comforted the women in these words: "Do not weep for me, weep for yourselves and for your children" (Lk 23:28).

Jesus was also thinking about others when he prepared the women and us for the suffering which might yet come to his followers: "If they do these things in the green wood what will happen in the dry?" (Lk 23:31). In effect, Jesus was saying: If innocence meets such a fate, what will be in store for the guilty?

As I lingered at this Station, I could hear Jesus still suffering in his body today. Business as usual was going on in the narrow street. Two men were threatening and accusing each other in a violent argument. A young boy was weeping uncontrollably. He was leading his donkey bearing crates of vegetables on its back when a rope broke, and the produce scattered over the alley-way that was called a street. I tried to comfort him by helping him gather up the load he was taking to the market-stall.

Pushing and jostling with no apparent consideration for others was going on all around me. The sellers were trying to drain every cent they could from the prospective buyer, while the buyers were bargaining without any thought of livelihood for the seller.

It was just another case of man's inhumanity to man, in spite of the fact that Jesus commanded us to love our neighbor as ourselves, and taught us by his own example how to love.

Today as we contemplate the Eighth Station we must remember that we are living with the risen, exalted, glorified Jesus. As we look back with him on this scene, we cannot help but be moved to a deep spirit of gratitude for all that he endured for us.

As he points to the loving compassion of "the Daughters of Jerusalem," a spirit of compassion wells up within us. Obviously, Jesus was pleased with their act of kindness.

Jesus points to so many similar situations in every city, town and village throughout the world. His Body is still on its Via Dolorosa. It still needs comfort and love. We can almost feel the pangs of loneliness and rejection, of fear and insecurity, of pain and suffering that people around us endure. How badly the Body of Jesus needs comfort and consolation, reassurance and love!

Jesus might remind us how easily we can reach out in loving concern to others. It may be a phone call to a shut-in, a personal visit, a thoughtful note, a simple gift. These are a few of the many avenues which open up to us each day.

The suffering Jesus is wending his way through our midst each day. Beg him to help you to recognize him, and to reach out to him as he comes to you in so many guises. Listen as he says: "I assure you, as often as you did it for one of my least brothers, you did it for me" (Mt 25:40).

FIFTEEN

Ninth Station
THIRD FALL

Hebrews 12: 1-13

The site of the third fall of Jesus under his cross is not found so easily. It is in a Coptic monastery. The ninth station is marked by a Roman column. It is near the apse of the Basilica of the Holy Sepulchre, and within sight of the place of execution.

The column which indicated this spot is not always apparent to the public. As I was searching out the spot where Jesus collapsed, I found a Coptic priest sitting there deeply engrossed in prayer. Even though we could not communicate verbally, he was very gracious and pointed out the column to me and also showed how close it is to Calvary. This monk invited me to rest, relax, and pray here at this site. I gladly welcomed the opportunity and the privilege.

My thoughts naturally turned to Jesus' determination to carry out fully and exactly the will of his Father. His strength was ebbing away, his limbs numbed with pain, yet as they dragged him to his feet after his third fall, he stumbled on toward the place of execution.

How frequently he told us that he had come into

the world to do the will of his Father. In this conviction he was singlehearted. It was his sole preoccupation. Even though this was the third time that he weakened and fell to the ground, he persisted in reaching the summit of Calvary. Jesus had taught: "The man who holds out to the end, however, is the one who will see salvation" (Mt 24:13). Jesus not only taught us the importance of perseverance, but he showed us by his own example.

One of the evil one's most common and most insidious temptations is to lead us into discouragement. He knows that if we get discouraged, we are simply not going to try. He is aware, too, that our prayer will begin to cool. Our relationship with the Lord will begin to wane. Fears, doubts, and anxieties will destroy our peace. We become self-centered. When we lose our focus on God, we become depressed more easily, and discouragement builds within us. The evil one is very clever in leading us into discouragement.

The author of the Letter to the Hebrews offers us some sage advice. He encourages us "to persevere in running the race which lies ahead; let us keep our eyes fixed on Jesus, who inspires and perfects our faith" (Heb 12:1-2).

When our focus is on Jesus our whole attitude begins to change. When we reflect on how he rose to his feet and persevered to the height of Calvary, leaving us his bloodstained footprints as an encouragement for us to follow, our crosses seem to become infinitesimally small.

The writer of Hebrews continues: "For the sake of the joy which lay before him he endured the cross, heedless of its shame. . . . Remember how he endured the opposition of sinners; hence do not grow despondent or abandon the struggle" (Heb 12:3).

How encouraging are these words in our daily struggle! Furthermore, we are not carrying our cross alone. Jesus promised: "Know that I am with you always, until the end of the world" (Mt 28:20).

Even if we seem to fail at times, there is no reason for discouragement. What appears to be a failure may be a means by which our loving Father intends to direct us into another and more fruitful channel of ministry. We have but to recall that if persecution had not broken out against the infant Church in Jerusalem, it would not have spread so rapidly into the world. God's plans are always mysterious.

History records countless cases when an apparent failure directed someone into a new apostolate which God had in mind for that person. In our own lives we can look back from the vantage point of time to see that a certain disappointment, or some tragic experience, or some so-called failure was a tremendous blessing in disguise.

Lord Jesus, grant me the courage and strength to rise after each new fall to walk faithfully and perseveringly in your footsteps.

SIXTEEN

Tenth Station
JESUS IS STRIPPED
OF HIS GARMENTS

Mark 10:17-31

The next stations are all found in the Chapel of
Golgotha. As you enter the Basilica of the Holy
Sepulchre, you will notice to the right a stairway
which leads to a Chapel about fifteen feet above the
main floor of the Basilica. This is the Chapel of Golgotha, the right side of which belongs to the Latin
Rite Christians, while the left belongs to the Greeks.
About one half of the floor of this Chapel rests on
the rock of Calvary. Beautiful mosaics depict the
scenes which took place here nearly two thousand
years ago.

Above the Latin altar we commemorate the tenth
station. Let us contemplate the event along with the
risen Jesus who is living with us and within us.

In preparation for his crucifixion Jesus was
stripped of his garments. What humiliation Jesus
must have suffered as the jeering mob ridiculed
him, especially in his helplessness and his naked-
ness.

This stripping caused him much physical pain, too. As they pulled off his clothes, many of the wounds of the scourging were torn open anew after the blood had congealed and imbedded his garments in the open wounds.

As we reflect on the happenings of this station, Jesus is teaching us the importance of detachment. Calvary is a lesson on detachment.

Jesus gave up his own will to conform precisely to the will of his Father. He gave us the person dearest to his heart — his Mother. Now he was giving up his own personal garments, especially the seamless robe, supposedly woven by his Mother.

Finally, he gave himself totally by breathing forth his life. This emptying was a total kenosis. There was nothing else to give. What a valuable lesson Jesus taught us!

On our spiritual journey back to the Father, we can be encumbered by many useless and unnecessary things, attachments which deflect our attention from our primary end. We can so easily lose our focus because we attach great importance to something which is relatively trivial.

Our greatest attachment is often our own will. We become accustomed to doing things our way. We set certain goals for ourselves, and sometimes goals for every one else as well.

Sometimes we need the approval of others. We cannot accept criticism. This too can be an attachment to our own ideas arising from our insecurity.

Even when we come to pray, we want, and sometimes demand, certain things from God. When our heart is attached, our mind is not free to enter into a close union with God in prayer. We need to come with complete openness. The ideal prayer posture before the Lord is: "Here I am, Lord, what is it you want?"

Jesus teaches us detachment when he said: "The foxes have lairs, the birds in the sky have nests, but the Son of Man has nowhere to lay his head" (Mt 8:20).

One of the gospel scenes points out the necessity of detachment. A rich man came to Jesus and wanted to be his disciple and to share in everlasting life. Jesus' advice was direct: "Go and sell what you have and give it to the poor. You will then have treasure in heaven. After that come and follow me" (Mk 10:17ff).

"Jesus looked at him with love. . . the man's face fell. He went away sad." Notice that this man was not at the foot of the cross on Calvary.

We are called to be apostles of the Good News. Our witness will be fruitful to the extent that we are detached from the things of this world. The detachment must be all-inclusive: fine clothes, expensive cars, the best in food and drink, and many, many lesser things.

Detachment includes even more than freedom from material things. It means a detachment from ourselves, our personal concerns, our hopes and ambitions. We cannot be a good listener unless we are completely detached.

Jesus was the best listener in all the world, because he had no worries, no anxieties, no personal hang-ups. We cannot be empathetic unless, like Jesus, we first empty ourselves.

As we contemplate this tenth station and see Jesus stripped of everything, detachment seems easier. Let us beg him for the grace to be totally detached.

SEVENTEEN

Eleventh Station
JESUS IS NAILED TO THE CROSS

Colossians 2:9-15

O ver the Latin altar on Calvary is a large mosaic depicting the three Marys standing at a little distance and painfully watching as Jesus is being nailed to the cross. Adjacent to this picture a portion of the mosaic shows the sacrifice of Isaac, which was a prototype of the sacrifice of Christ.

As one contemplates this sorrowful scene, the theme which seems to prevail is one of total submission on the part of Jesus. He was completely submissive to his Father's will. He submitted to the soldiers as they carried out their cruel task of impaling him to the cross.

Jesus could be submissive because he knew what his cross would do for a fallen world. He also understood why his Father willed it so.

Paul with his usual clarity sums up the reconciliation won for us in these words: "It pleased God to make absolute fullness reside in him and by means of him, to reconcile everything in his person, both on earth and in the heavens, making peace through the blood of his cross" (Col 1:19-20). The apostle of the Gentiles explains how reconciliation was won for us. "He cancelled the bond that stood against us with all its claims, snatching it up and nailing it to the cross" (Col 2:14).

Jesus knew the secret of the cross. He was well aware of the power hidden in that cross. It was a power sufficiently potent to disarm the principalities and powers; the power to reclaim a fallen race.

There is so much mystery here that our finite minds are incapable of grasping its full implications. Nevertheless, from this mystery enough clarity has emerged to inspire, to motivate, to strengthen, to support the followers of Jesus throughout the ages and lead them to submit to their own personal nailing to the cross.

In the charter of Christianity which Jesus proclaimed in his Sermon on the Mount, he explained to us that persecution would be the lot of his disciples. He added another dimension: not only that his followers should expect persecution, but that they should accept it willingly and joyfully.

How succinctly, but how emphatically Jesus set forth this tenet of his way of life:

> Blest are those persecuted for holiness' sake:
>   the reign of God is theirs.
> Blest are you when they insult you and persecute you and utter every kind of slander against you because of me.
> Be glad and rejoice, for your reward is great in heaven! they have persecuted the prophets before you in the same way (Mt 5:10-12).

The years have proved Jesus was right. Down through the ages joy has always been the badge of the martyrs.

Jesus not only taught us in word, but showed us by his own way of life. In another context Jesus said: "What I just did was to give you an example: as I have done, so you must do" (Jn 13:15).

It is true that Jesus said this about his being willing to serve rather than be served, but surely it has a universal application.

The example of Jesus, along with his grace, enabled Stephen, the first martyr, to accept martyrdom joyfully and with the same mentality that Jesus had toward his persecutors. "Lord, do not hold this sin against them" (Acts 7:60).

Some centuries later, as Thomas More was being beheaded, he pulled his beard aside so that it would not be severed by the executioner's blade and jokingly remarked that his beard was not guilty of treason.

Countless other martyrs throughout the ages have met death with peace and joy, some even singing to the very end.

In the meantime, pain, suffering, martyrdom of all sorts goes on behind the iron and bamboo curtains, in many other countries of the world, in our abortion clinics, on our city streets.

How can we explain this paradox? It is impossible to understand why persecution must go on until we contemplate Jesus being nailed to the cross. Only then does it begin to make sense in this jigsaw puzzle of life.

We can never resolve this mystery, but after reflecting and pondering the eleventh station, we can begin to understand why Jesus called the persecuted "blessed" and why he could say: "Be glad and rejoice."

EIGHTEEN

Twelfth Station
THE DEATH OF JESUS

Matthew 27: 35-50

On the left side of the Chapel of Golgotha the Greeks have erected a marble altar over the cleft in the rock into which the cross of Jesus was inserted. Under the altar there is a disk about fifteen inches above the floor. You may insert your hand into the hole in the disk and touch the rock with its cleft. This is how the place of execution appears today.

When Jesus was led to his death, he was taken outside the city to a place near the city walls. Here a rocky knoll jutted out and his cross was implanted so that those passing by on the roadway could see him. Exposing their victim to the public gaze was another way in which his enemies could gloat over their apparent victory.

It was evening when I arrived at the Chapel of Golgotha to spend some time in prayer. The sun was beginning its downward arc toward the horizon. It made some strange shadows here in the Chapel. It reminded me of the darkness of the first Good Friday. "From noon onward, there was darkness over the whole land until midafternoon" (Mt 27:45).

A strange coincidence occurred. The rays of the slanting sun coming through the windows cast the shadow of a huge cross on the floor of the chapel. Inadvertently I had come to pray in the shadow of the cross.

Since Jesus obediently accepted death on the cross, the cross has become a standard around which we rally. It is the symbol of the greatest love a person can have, to lay down his life for his friends. The cross is our comfort and consolation. It gives us hope and reassurance in this land of exile.

The cross is a sacred sign and symbol for all Christians. For two thousand years men and women have come in endless procession to that cross.

Throughout the ages countless persons have come to bask in the shadow of Jesus' cross which has been erected on the steeples of our churches, on public buildings, on the walls of our homes or in the hands of the sick and suffering. They have all come to seek comfort and consolation, peace and joy, in the shadow of the cross.

Sinners like ourselves have come, because we realize that our sins have been nailed to that cross. By means of that cross peace has been restored to our souls and we are reunited with our loving Father.

As sinners we come to plead: "Lord, remember me when you enter your reign." His compassionate response is always the same: "I assure you: this day you will be with me in paradise" (Lk 23:42).

The dying lie at the foot of his cross. Death is inevitable because of sin, but because of his death on the cross, death for us has become the doorway into an eternal union with him, a union of perfect love.

Those who are suffering come to weep in the shadow of that cross. There they realize that there is not a single pain which he has not already endured, and which he has not sanctified.

The homeless come and kneel at the foot of that cross and as they gaze they realize that he, too, was homeless, with nowhere to lay his head.

The lonely come and kneel silently before him. Here they realize that he was the loneliest man in all the world. He knew the loneliness of death, the loneliness of being apparently abandoned by his Father. In the shadow of the cross loneliness becomes more tolerable.

I, too, can come to the cross to hear those consoling words: "Your sins are forgiven you."

I can come when I find it hard to forgive because I am hurt, wronged, or misunderstood. I listen as I hear him pray: "Father, forgive them: they do not know what they are doing" (Lk 23-34).

I can come when I feel lonely and discouraged in my ministry; when no one seems interested. In the shadow of the cross I can hear Jesus say to me: "Do not let your hearts be troubled. Have faith in God and faith in me" (Jn 14:1).

I can come when I feel weary and exhausted, and there realize how true are his words: "Come to me, all you who are weary and find life burdensome, and I will refresh you" (Mt 11:28).

I can come to the cross to listen to the message of

love which speaks more eloquently than words, the message which every human heart longs to hear repeatedly: "As the Father has loved me, so I have loved you" (Jn 15:9).

The sun had set and the shadow of the cross disappeared off the floor. I wanted to linger longer in the peaceful shadow of the cross, but I knew that I could find the cross wherever my path would lead me.

NINETEEN

Thirteenth Station
JESUS' BODY
TAKEN OFF THE CROSS

John 19: 38-40

After we had offered the eucharistic sacrifice at the altar commemorating the Tenth and Eleventh Stations, we paused for a time in reflection and prayer at the little altar marking the Thirteenth Station. This altar is situated between the two main altars on Calvary and is only an arm's length from either altar.

Over this altar is a beautiful statue of our Sorrowful Mother, carved in wood. This statue depicts the grief of Mary as Jesus is taken down from the cross. It was carved in the sixteenth or seventeenth century and was sent to Jerusalem from Lisbon in 1778.

The Thirteenth Station commemorates the natural sequel to John's brief statement of Mary's role on Calvary. "Near the cross of Jesus there stood his mother. ." (John 19:25). In this brief statement there is summed up a lifetime of loving dedication and unflinching commitment.

Note that John emphasizes that Mary *stood*. She did not swoon, overcome with grief, even though her suffering must have been greater than any other mother's pain at the loss of a son in death. Mary was sinless; hence she understood more keenly the envy, the hatred, the rejection which nailed her Son to the cross of infamy.

The blasphemy, the insults, the mockery, and gloating which rose like a mighty crescendo must have pierced her heart to its very depths.

After Jesus said, "Now it is finished," and after "he bowed his head and delivered over his spirit," Joseph of Arimathea and Nicodemus reverently and lovingly took his body down from the cross.

For a brief time Mary held that broken and bruised body in her arms. Michelangelo has immortalized this scene in his masterful work, the Pieta. The Pieta is not only a masterpiece of art; it is also a powerful incentive to prayer and dedication.

Years earlier, Mary held the body of her Infant Son to her heart as she poured out her love upon him. Now that body is returned to her rejected, broken, a victim of our sinfulness.

Mary continues to envelop his body in love. She can count, in every wound, in every laceration, an expression of the love of her Son for sinful mankind. The sharp edge of Simeon's predicted sword was penetrating more deeply into her Immaculate Heart.

Mary willingly accepted this sword of sorrow because her commitment, made some thirty years earlier, was without reservation. Mary could not possibly have foreseen nor understood what was in store for her when she graciously uttered her *Fiat*.

I am sure that Mary often recalled how often she

had heard her Son say that he had come to do the will of his Father. He was single-minded in this resolve even unto death.

And what was the will of the Father? "Yes, God so loved the world that he gave his only Son, that whoever believes in him may not die but have eternal life. God did not send the Son into the world to condemn the world, but that the world might be saved through him" (Jn 3:16:17).

Mary made her commitment in love. She did not weigh the cost of discipleship, nor did she explore the ramifications of her commitment before she gave her consent. Her love was so intense that she had to give everything.

What a comfort for all of us to know that we have a spiritual Mother who has experienced suffering and pain, a Mother who understands every heartache and pain which could ever come our way. We have a Mother whose chief concern is that not a single drop of the precious blood of her Son be spilled in vain.

In her oblation on Calvary, Mary offered the pain of every mother's heart. Mary knows how dreadful is the suffering which mothers endure in the loss of a son, especially when a son is lost in a traffic fatality, in the slaughter of war, by suicide, or through the brutality of man's inhumanity to man.

We sing "At the cross her station keeping" and we know that at our side, she also keeps her perpetual vigil. That is why Jesus gave her to us on Calvary.

TWENTY

Fourteenth Station
JESUS IS BURIED

John 19:38-42

O ne of the most sacred spots in Jerusalem is the site of the burial and resurrection of Jesus. The burial place of Jesus is housed within its own chapel in the Basilica of the Holy Sepulchre. It is the focal point of the whole Basilica, not only because of its strategic geographical location, but in virtue of the tremendous mystery which it represents to all Christians.

Near the grave of Jesus, in an adjoining room, one can see, even today, many burial places hewn out of the rock. These graves could very easily date back to the time of Jesus.

After Jesus had died, Joseph of Arimathea and Nicodemus asked Pilate for permission to remove the body of Jesus from the cross to bury it. Scripture speaks highly of these two disciples. Joseph of Arimathea is described as "a distinguished member of the Sanhedrin" (Mk 15:43). Luke tells us of Joseph of Arimathea in these words: "There was a man named Joseph, an upright and holy member of the Sanhedrin, who had not been associated with their plan or their action. He was from Arimathea, a Jewish town, and looked expectantly for the reign of God" (Lk 23:50-51).

We first meet Nicodemus in John 3:1. "A Pharisee, named Nicodemus, a member of the Jewish Sanhedrin, came to him at night...." Nicodemus questioned Jesus about his teachings. As a result of these nocturnal meetings we are indebted to Nicodemus for a much better understanding of the significance of Baptism.

Both of these disciples were brave men. It took courage to admit their discipleship at the time when Jesus apparently had gone down in utter defeat. It was not safe to be a disciple at that moment. It could mean persecution and death. Yet these two disciples risked the danger of arrest and punishment, perhaps even death, to do what their love called them to do for Jesus. Furthermore, they opened themselves to ridicule and rejection from their peers among the Jewish leaders, as well as from the general populace.

But nothing daunted these men because they had learned to love Jesus. Love never looks at the price tag. When the Lord is our first priority, nothing else really matters.

By this act of kindness they were publicly announcing that they were disciples of Jesus, and that they did not concur with nor condone the injustice perpetrated by the Sanhedrin.

Nicodemus manifested his love by a generous gift. "Nicodemus likewise came, bringing a mixture of myrrh and aloes which weighed about a hundred pounds" (Jn 19:39).

Joseph's gift to Jesus was his own grave. "Taking the body, Joseph wrapped it in fresh linen and laid it in his own new tomb which had been hewn from a formation of rock" (Mt 27:59).

These two disciples are a great source of inspiration and encouragement for us. They set us a challenging example.

The Body of Christ needs loving care and concern. We see this on all sides of us. In times of tragedy, serious illness, and especially when death visits our family or friends, we have a splendid opportunity to reach out in loving concern to others.

There are times when words cannot possibly express our deepest feelings of empathy, but our presence speaks volumes. We become channels of Jesus' loving concern by permitting him to flow through us to our brothers and sisters who are in need.

Unfortunately, in our day of speed and hurried confusion, time seems to be at a premium. Perhaps we need to reexamine our priorities and set them in order once again.

Did you ever think about calling on Joseph of Arimathea or Nicodemus to intercede for you that you might develop a courageous, sympathetic, understanding heart?

TWENTY-ONE

JESUS GOES TO DINNER

Luke 7:36-50

Jesus experienced rejection in many different forms. Sometimes he encountered open hostility. At other times rejection came in the form of slander, trying to discredit him. At times the rejection was subtle and insidious.

Let us ponder one of the many rejections which Jesus received throughout his lifetime. Jesus was invited to dinner by Simon, a Pharisee. We do not really know the reason for the invitation. Many different reasons have been suggested. It seems that Simon was eager to meet anyone who was considered a celebrity, or was on the road to fame. With a half-patronizing contempt, Simon invited Jesus, this startling young Galilean, to have a meal with him. In this way Simon tried to patronize Jesus.

During the course of the dinner a sinful woman came in and went right to Jesus. Simon's eyebrows must have been raised, for he was thinking: "If this man were a prophet, he would know who and what sort of woman this is that touches him — that she is a sinner."

Jesus read Simon's thoughts. "In answer to his thoughts, Jesus said to him, 'Simon, I have something to propose to you.' " In mock courtesy and feigned eagerness Simon said: "Teacher, speak."

Jesus then gently but firmly pointed out to Simon the many discourtesies by which he was rejecting Jesus. The roads were dusty, and open sandals were the only footwear used at that time. Cool water was always poured over the feet of a guest to cleanse and soothe them. Jesus reminded Simon, although Simon was well aware of the fact: "I came to your home and you provided me with no water for my feet."

The host always extended to his guest the kiss of peace. This was a mark of respect which was never omitted, especially to a distinguished rabbi. Jesus gently reminded Simon: "You gave me no kiss." Not to welcome a guest with a Shalom was a subtle method of rejection.

There was another courtesy which Simon did not extend to Jesus. It was customary to anoint a person's hair with sweet-smelling oil. Again Jesus recalled this neglect to Simon: "You did not anoint my head with oil."

In this case not one of these three courtesies were offered to Jesus. In the culture of that day, that meant rejection. Jesus graciously accepted that rejection and went on quietly trying to touch Simon's heart.

There was an even greater rejection on Simon's part. Jesus was trying to teach Simon a lesson on sinfulness and forgiveness. However, Simon did not see himself in the story of the two debtors. Simon was not conscious of any need for forgiveness; therefore, he did not receive forgiveness from God. Simon's impression of himself was that he was a good man in God's sight and also in the sight of men.

On the other hand, the sinful woman recognized not only her need for forgiveness, but she also recognized in Jesus a God who could forgive sin. She was overwhelmed by his love for her in spite of her sinfulness. She knew he could forgive and she humbly came to ask for that forgiveness.

One thing which will shut a man off from God is his own self-sufficiency. It is strange that the closer a person comes to God, the more he recognizes his sinfulness and his need for forgiveness. Paul could speak of sinners "of these I myself am the worst" (1 Tm 1:15). St. Francis of Assisi could say: "There is nowhere a more wretched and a more miserable sinner than I."

It is true to say that the greatest of sins is to be conscious of no sin. A sense of need will open the door to God's forgiveness, because God is love, and love's greatest glory is to be needed.

In other words, Simon rejected the forgiving, healing, redeeming love which Jesus extended to him. Simon rejected Jesus as God, One who longed to forgive sins.

Contemplating this event gives us reason to pause, to ponder, and reflect on our own attitude.

With the blind man let us pray: "Be merciful to me a sinner."

TWENTY-TWO

JESUS REJECTED
IN THE EUCHARIST

John 6:60-69

Throughout his whole life Jesus experienced the pain of rejection. One of the most pathetic rejections was the refusal of the disciples to accept the gift of himself in the Eucharist.

The sequence of events came in this way. There were times when Jesus desired to withdraw from the crowds. He was under constant strain and needed rest. Moreover, he wanted to be alone with his disciples to teach them privately and lead them into a deeper understanding of himself. Furthermore, he needed time alone for prayer.

Jesus left Capernaum and sailed the four miles to the other side of the Lake. The people watched him leave and went north over the fords of the Jordan and arrived at Bethsaida Julias.

When the crowds arrived, they had no food. Jesus fed them with five barley loaves and a few dried fish. When the crowd witnessed this sign, they wanted to carry him off and make him king. Jesus fled to the other side of the Lake and back to Capernaum.

The next day the crowd found him. He chided them with: "I assure you, you are not looking for me because you have seen signs but because you have eaten your fill of the loaves. You should not be working for perishable food, but for food that remains unto life eternal, food which the Son of Man will give you" (Jn 6:26-27).

When the crowd begged: "Give us this bread always," Jesus explained to them in detail the spiritual food of the Eucharist which he was about to give them. This was too much for them. They would not accept his words.

The evangelist uses some pathetic words to describe their reactions. "This sort of talk is hard to endure! How can anyone take it seriously?" And then John continues: "From that time on, many of his disciples broke away and would not remain in his company any longer."

I was sitting one evening on the ruined walls of the synagogue in Capernaum meditating on these words. The evening breeze coming off the Sea of Galilee was refreshing. I heard the trudging of many feet coming from behind me. A group of tourists arrived, gave a few casual glances at the ruins of what was Capernaum. Then I heard the tour guide remark: "Some Christians believe that Jesus of Nazareth came here to live and that he taught some of his truths here." That was the end of the explanation and they left.

It jarred me for a moment. I was tempted to call after them and tell them more of Capernaum, but then I remembered what Jesus did. He let them go.

In fact, he even went farther. Jesus turned to the

Twelve and said: "Do you want to leave me too?"
There must have been a moment of hushed silence,
then Peter broke the silence with that refreshing:
"Lord, to whom shall we go? You have the words of
eternal life." Yes, Jesus was willing to let them go, if
they did not want to believe what he had just explained to them.

The rejection goes on daily in spite of the great
gift which Jesus is offering. Many whom he has
called into discipleship are breaking away and are
no longer remaining in his company. We hear such
expressions as: "I don't get anything out of the
Mass" or "The Mass is not meaningful for me."

In our age we have become intoxicated with our
own intellectual prowess. In our technological society, man has become a god unto himself. He does
not see the need for a God of love. He has become
self-sufficient. It is hard for the pride of modern
man to accept Jesus' words literally. Jesus always
asked for a lively faith, a trusting faith, a faith of
commitment.

At times I wonder if we lack the faith to believe,
or if we find that the way of life which Jesus ex-
pounded is too difficult for us to follow.

As I sat there on the ruins of the synagogue I
could almost hear the pleading words of Jesus being
wafted along the evening breeze: "Do you want to
leave me too?"

I thanked him for the grace to say with Peter:
"Lord, to whom shall we go? You have the words of
eternal life."

TWENTY-THREE

MOUNT TABOR

Luke 9:28–36

It was a beautiful, balmy spring morning when we began our pilgrimage to the summit of Mount Tabor. The road leading to the top is steep and narrow, with numerous switchbacks beckoning the pilgrim onward. It takes an hour of hard climbing to reach the top.

Jesus chose Mt. Tabor as the ideal place to reveal more about himself and his mission of suffering to his apostles. Mt. Tabor is a sugarloaf mountain rising up alone in the plains of Esdraelon. Its summit is 1,500 feet above the valley floor. The mountain forms a perfect altar under the beautiful canopy of heaven.

This is one of the most picturesque spots in Israel with a commanding view of the fertile valley below, Mt. Hermon forming a backdrop to the north and Mt. Gerazim on the south. The mountain forms an altar in the midst of the sanctuary of Israel. Little wonder that Jesus chose this place to bring his three favorite apostles to spend time in prayer, and also to prepare them for his mission of redemption.

The apostles needed this taboric experience. The

time of the death of Jesus was rapidly approaching. Jesus knew that all would be scandalized in him. They would be filled with confusion and consternation when they saw their Messiah go down in utter defeat. Their expectation of a Messiah was diametrically different than what God had in mind.

For this reason Jesus took his favorite apostles to the summit of Mt. Tabor, so that they could experience the splendor of his divinity radiating through his humanity.

What an experience this must have been for the apostles! Luke says: "The disciples kept quiet, telling nothing of what they had seen at that time to anyone." Some experiences in life are too other-worldly to be expressed in words.

The disciples needed this confirmation of Jesus' divinity so that they could in turn strengthen the tottering faith of others. How often God does the same for us! He reveals himself, his paternal concern, his love, his awareness of our problems, to strengthen us in our faith.

The Father wanted us to know that the passion and death of Jesus was all in accord with his divine plan. Once again he wanted to confirm the mission of Jesus, as he had done at his baptism in the River Jordan. Thus the Father confirmed his mission of suffering by assuring us: "This is my beloved Son on whom my favor rests," and then the command: "Listen to him."

The apostles needed to hear the Father's confirmation of the mission of the Suffering Servant because their concept of the Messiah had to be revised. This is just another way of the Father saying: "For my thoughts are not your thoughts, nor are your ways my ways" (Is 55:8).

Luke makes a point of telling us that they "went up onto the mountain to pray. While he was praying his face changed in appearance. . ."

I find two valuable lessons in that fact. In the first place Jesus met his Father in prayer and in that prayer he was able to accept his mission of dreadful suffering and death. Furthermore, only with that acceptance in prayer was Jesus transfigured before their eyes. When Jesus was able to say "Yes" to the Father, then his divinity shone forth through his humanity.

Note too that Luke says they were "at prayer." In prayer we will come to know Jesus better. As we spend time in contemplating his love and goodness we will get new insights and a deeper understanding of him as a Person. Only then can we get to know him with our hearts. In prayer we will not only get to know Jesus as he is "transfigured" in our lives, but we will begin to understand that his ways are not our ways. We will be better enabled to say our "Yes" to whatever he asks of us.

As we get to know this deeper dimension of who Jesus is, we will be able to love him more intensely. When we experience his love in this richer way, then we cannot help but be totally his.

As he is revealed more personally to us in prayer we can sincerely say with Peter: "Master, how good it is for us to be here."

TWENTY-FOUR

First Word
"FATHER FORGIVE THEM"

Luke 23:34

The Church of the Holy Sepulchre which houses the Calvary chapel is a very busy place. Pilgrims are milling about everywhere. There are a number and a variety of liturgical celebrations going on in different Rites. Calvary is not the quietest place for prayer during the day. However, I discovered that the very early morning hours were quiet; peaceful and still.

Early one morning in the semi-light I nestled in my favorite corner to be alone with the Lord. As I was getting comfortable, Jesus' words spoken from the cross rang in my mind: "Father forgive them; they do not know what they are doing."

These words give us another aspect of the portrait of Jesus. He said and taught many wonderful things, but rarely anything more wonderful than these words. What comfort and what joy they bring to our hearts!

Jesus was not only praying for his executioners, not only for great sinners, but he was praying for all of us. In the original language of John's gospel, the imperfect tense of the verb is used, which means that Jesus kept repeating over and over again: "Father, forgive them; they do not know what they are doing." It also implies that, throughout the centuries, Jesus has been interceding with the Father for us, in the same words.

Jesus not only prays to his Father to forgive us, but he excuses our waywardness. He tells the Father that, due to the weakness of our human nature and the lack of awareness of the malice of our sins, we should be forgiven. He was thinking of us when he said: "they do not know what they are doing."

Jesus not only taught us that we should have a forgiving heart, but he also showed us the way by his own example. Even in death, he excuses his executioners.

There is nothing more beautiful, nothing more rare, than Christian forgiveness. Forgiveness is an amazing thing.

Stephen, one of the first deacons of the early church, had learned well the Christian attitude which Jesus formed in his disciples. As Stephen was about to be stoned to death he prayed for his executioners: "Lord, do not hold this sin against them" (Acts 7:60).

Paul, who had been taught and transformed by Jesus himself, urged the early Christians to have a forgiving heart at all times. He writes: "Be kind to one another, compassionate, and mutually forgiving, just as God has forgiven you in Christ" (Eph 4:32).

Jesus pleaded with his Father to forgive because, as he said, the people were acting out of ignorance.

This same thought prevails throughout the New Testament. Peter explained to the people: "Yet I know, my brothers, that you acted out of ignorance, just as your leaders did" (Acts 3:17). Paul also maintains that they crucified Jesus because they did not know him (Acts 13:27).

Forgiveness is the very essence of the Christian way of life which Jesus set up for us to follow. An unforgiving spirit can make us a bitter, resentful person. An unforgiving spirit will quickly rob us of the peace and joy, the tranquillity and serenity which Jesus wants us to have. It hardens our hearts so that his divine life and love cannot radiate through us to others.

When we find it hard to reach out in loving forgiveness to others who have harmed us, when we cannot seem to forgive them from the depths of our being, perhaps it might be well for us to revisit Calvary.

There, as we sit in the shadow of the cross, listen to the blasphemy and insults, the derision and hatred leveled at Jesus while he hangs helpless on that deathbed of a cross. Above the gloating and the terrible taunts hurled at him, hear his voice loud and clear: "Father, forgive them; they do not know what they are doing."

And remember, he died praying for you and me.

TWENTY-FIVE

Second Word
THE PROMISE OF PARADISE

Luke 23:39-43

It does not seem to be a mere coincidence that Jesus was crucified between two known criminals. This was purposely and deliberately so planned in order to humiliate Jesus even more, in front of his disciples and before the general populace, and to rank him with criminals.

Even though this might have been done maliciously, God could still use it for his own purposes. Jesus was always a friend of sinners, why should he not die in their midst?

It also gave Jesus the occasion to reach out in merciful compassion to win another soul for his kingdom. God can use even the perfidy of man to accomplish his will.

There are many legends about the penitent thief. One legend makes him a Judaean Robin Hood who robbed the rich to give to the poor. Another, that he was instrumental in protecting the Holy Family on their journey into Egypt against an attack by robbers.

Someone else has said that, true to form, he was a

robber until the end, because he stole heaven.

The original language implies that the thief asked Jesus frequently to remember him when he entered into his kingdom. This proved the sincerity of his asking for forgiveness, and of his genuine conversion.

Here again we come to know Jesus a little better. He is a God of loving compassion and merciful forgiveness. Jesus did not exact a formal expression of sorrow, nor did he point to the thief's past transgressions, even though they were so great that they were punishable by death. All that was important to Jesus was the man's present disposition; the sacrament of the moment, if you will. The thief's whole attitude of mind and heart was summarized in his plea: "Jesus, remember me when you enter upon your reign."

What hope, what joy, what consolation, what comfort, what reassurance Jesus brought to this outcast of society when he gave him that extravagant promise: "I assure you: this day you will be with me in Paradise."

Jesus' reply to the good thief were the last words which he spoke to any person on earth.

Jesus did not merely promise him a remembrance in his kingdom, nor did he promise that he would gain entrance only. No, Jesus' promise implied much more.

The word "Paradise" is a Persian word meaning "a walled garden." When a Persian king wished to do one of his subjects a very special honor he made him a companion, on a walk in the king's garden.

By his use of the word "Paradise," Jesus was

promising the thief more than immortality. He promised him the honored place of a companion of the garden in the courts of heaven. Jesus promised that the thief would not merely be in his retinue, but that he would be sharing his royalty.

With these few words Jesus manifested once again the infinite mercy of God. Speaking to us through Ezekiel, God assures us: "I take no pleasure in the death of the wicked man, but rather in the wicked man's conversion, that he may live" (Ez 33:11).

The psalmist, too, reminds us of God's merciful love and what joy it brings us: "Happy is he whose fault is taken away, whose sin is covered" (Ps 32:1).

As I pondered these encouraging words of Jesus in the dim light of the predawn in the chapel on Calvary, I recalled the power of his words. As the sacred writer puts it: "God's word is living and effective, sharper than a two-edged sword" (Heb 4:12).

In my introspection I asked myself, is God's Word of mercy and forgiveness alive and active in me, so that I am a source of hope and encouragement to others, especially those who are seeking his merciful forgiveness?

Is my sensitivity such that in spite of misunderstanding, abuse or even hatred, I can reach out to others with the gentleness of the Heart of Jesus?

As I strive each day with the help of his grace to become "gentle and humble of heart," I am certain that someday I shall hear those joyous words addressed to me: "this day you will be with me in Paradise."

TWENTY-SIX

Third Word
"THERE IS YOUR MOTHER"

John 19:25-27

A small Greek altar, beautifully ornamented in Eastern style, stands over the cleft in the rock in which, it is claimed, the cross of Jesus was inserted. The reredos is ornately decorated in the style of the Oriental Rite. An almost life-sized icon of Mary stands beneath the cross, as John says: "Near the cross of Jesus there stood his mother."

In the dim light of early morning, the halo surrounding the head and face of Mary was beginning to radiate its silvery brightness. As I gazed on the face of Mary, whose eyes were fixed on Jesus, I reflected how the words of Jesus must have affected her.

In two brief statements, Jesus manifested his loving concern for his Mother and for his Church. "Woman, there is your son," and "There is your mother." In these few but tender words, Jesus presented his Mother to John's care, and John to Mary's.

From a human point of view, there is something infinitely moving in the fact that in his dying moments Jesus thought of the loneliness of his Mother, in the days which lay ahead after his death.

What a gift Jesus gave to John and to us: "There is your mother." Mary would be the source of comfort and consolation to John and to us after Jesus' work on earth was completed.

Magnanimous as this gift of filial piety was, there is much more contained in this mutual exchange. Mary accepted the exchange, a human son for a divine Son. True to her total dedication in love she accepted even more, the spiritual motherhood of the whole Church. All this is implied in these few words of Jesus.

The glorification of Jesus on the cross enacted a totally new relationship between us and God. By his death and resurrection, Jesus reestablished our union with him. We are members of his body; we are one with Jesus. He is living with us and within us.

Mary is not only the Mother of Jesus, but by her cooperation in the mystery of salvation she has entered into a spiritual motherhood of the whole Church.

In a singular way Mary participated in the mystery of our redemption by her unqualified obedience and her deep faith. She was not only passively present at the events of our salvation, but she lovingly consented to the immolation of the Son she herself brought forth. Jesus declared blessed those who hear the word of God and keep it. Mary was doing just that when she united her will, painful as the occasion was, to the salvific will of God.

The Second Vatican Council teaches: "She

(Mary) is our Mother in the order of grace. This maternity of Mary in the order of grace began with the consent which she gave in faith at the Annunciation and which she sustained without wavering beneath the cross, and lasts until the eternal fulfillment of all the elect" (Constitution on the Church, par. 62).

Under the cross of Calvary, John is our representative. Jesus gave his Mother to the Church through his beloved apostle. As Mother of the Church, Mary is concerned about my personal welfare, as well as that of the universal Church.

Jesus had already manifested to us the power of Mary's intercessory prayer. At the wedding feast in Cana, he responded to her request and worked the first of his signs, even though "his hour" had not yet come.

Immediately after the Ascension of Jesus into heaven, Mary is found again in her intercessory role with the infant Church. Luke tells us of the gathering of the disciples in the cenacle. After the Ascension the disciples returned to Jerusalem and "entering the city, they went to the upstairs room where they were staying. . . . Together they devoted themselves to constant prayer. There were some women in their company, and Mary the mother of Jesus and his brothers" (Acts 1:13f).

By her powerful prayers Mary was imploring upon the disciples the outpouring of the Holy Spirit — the same Spirit who had already overshadowed her in the Annunciation. Again her prayers were answered in a most extraordinary way.

My heart was filled with joy and gratitude, but

the only words which came to my lips were "Thank you, Mary, for being our Mother. Thank you for being my Mother!"

TWENTY-SEVEN

Fourth Word
"I AM THIRSTY"

John 19:28

Jesus suffered intensely every pain to which the human body is susceptible. He experienced the excruciating pain of thirst.

Jesus had lost a great quantity of blood in his cruel scourging. He was completely dehydrated. His tongue and throat were parched. In his extreme pain he cried out: "I am thirsty!"

There is little doubt that this thirst caused Jesus great physical pain. However the cry of Jesus has a much broader significance.

John says that Jesus said "I am thirsty," to fulfill the scripture. In a prophetic utterance the psalmist anticipated this suffering of Jesus in these words:

"Insult has broken my heart, and I am weak,
    I looked for sympathy, but there was none.
Rather they put gall in my food,

94

and in my thirst they gave me vinegar to
drink" (Psalm 69:21f).

And in another psalm this suffering of Jesus is
foretold:

"My throat is dried up like baked clay,
 my tongue cleaves to my jaws:
to the dust of death you have brought me down"
 (Psalm 22:16).

The evangelist also tells us that the soldiers used
hyssop to offer Jesus some common wine. This too is
significant. Hyssop was not the most practical
material to use for this purpose, but it reflects an
important connection.

Recall that the chosen people were ordered to eat
the passover lamb and sprinkle the doorposts of
their homes with its blood, using a piece of hyssop,
so that they would be spared the last plague in
Egypt. By using the word, "hyssop," John is point-
ing to Jesus as the true Passover Lamb.

Jesus suffered all the distress and the pain of
physical thirst for many reasons. Consequently, we
can draw many spiritual inferences from his dreadful thirst.

Jesus loves every person with an infinite love. His
heart was burning with love for every single one of
his creatures. At this peak of the pouring out his
love, he was thirsting for love in return. Love is
mutual. Love seeks only love in return.

He may have realized that throughout the ages
there would be countless men and women who
would not even pause to reflect on his love, or even
be aware of the great love with which he is reaching

out to them. This must have intensified his great thirst.

On the other hand, Jesus could foresee the many who would strive to return his love. He must have been comforted by all the men and women who would commit themselves totally in love to his call.

A second important reflection is the truth that every human heart would thirst for the love, the peace, and the joy which only God could give. Jesus longs to satisfy this thirst.

Jesus tried to explain to us through the Samaritan woman how he was going to quench our thirst. Through his death on the cross Jesus gave us the living water of his divine life.

This is how Jesus explained his life-giving gift to us:

> "Everyone who drinks this water
>   will be thirsty again.
> But whoever drinks the water I give him
>   will never be thirsty:
>   no, the water I give
>   shall become a fountain within him,
>   leaping up to provide eternal life"
> (John 4:13-14).

Jesus taught us that it is a special gift to hunger and thirst for this living water.

> "Blest are they who hunger and thirst
>   for holiness: they shall have their fill" (Mt. 5:6)

Do I really thirst to share more deeply the life of Christ?

How do I hunger and thirst for holiness?

TWENTY-EIGHT

Fifth Word
"MY GOD, MY GOD, WHY HAVE YOU FORSAKEN ME?"

Matthew 27:45-50

The stillness of the early morning silence in the chapel on Calvary seemed to ring and reecho with the cry of Jesus: "My God, my God, why have you forsaken me?"

At first we may be startled at this seemingly despairing cry of Jesus, until we realize that it is not a cry of interior abandonment, but that Jesus is crying out in the words of Psalm 22. It is not so much a cry of anguish as it is a prophecy fulfilled.

It is interesting to note how the whole psalm runs throughout the crucifixion narrative. These words of Jesus are actually the first verse of the psalm. Other verses follow in the gospel narrative.

Some suggest that at this very moment, the weight of the sins of the whole world became apparent to Jesus. Paul writes: "For our sakes God made him who did not know sin to be sin, so that in him we might become the very holiness of God" (2 Cor. 5:21). At that moment Jesus experienced the separation from God which sin brings. If this is the

97

case, it is a mystery at which we can only wonder.

On the other hand, there may be a more human explanation here. Jesus was truly human, and he would not be fully human unless he had plumbed to the uttermost depths all human experiences.

We may be immersed in an experience beyond our understanding. It may be a situation in which we experience a complete absence of God. It seemed to me in prayer that this is what happened to Jesus here on the cross.

In the Garden of Olives, Jesus knew only that he had to go on because it was the will of his Father. He had to accept it, and he willingly did so, though he did not understand it.

Now on the cross, Jesus is plumbing the very depths of the human condition, so that there would be no place that we might go where Jesus has not already been before. We are never asked to accept anything which Jesus himself did not experience. He showed us the way.

As I sat there in the peaceful quiet of Calvary, I remembered that Jesus did not die with this cry of anguish on his lips. Matthew tells us: "Once again Jesus cried out with a loud voice, and then gave up his spirit" (Mt 27:50).

The great shout is a victor's shout, according to all the evangelists. It is a cry of a man who has successfully accomplished a difficult task. It is the cry of a man who has conquered after a terrible struggle. It is the cry of a person who has grasped the crown. Jesus died a victor, with a shout of triumph on his lips.

Note, too, that Jesus willingly gave up his spirit.

As he had said earlier, no one takes his life from him, he willingly is handing it over for the salvation of the world.

As the words of Jesus lingered in my heart and mind, I asked myself, how do I respond to loneliness, desolation, or dryness in prayer?

In moments of trial do I question God's will, or do I reach out with the trust and confidence which Jesus had toward the Father?

How do I respond to the lonely, to those who are depressed or discouraged?

Life was beginning to stir here in the Calvary chapel. Devout pilgrims were beginning to arrive to venerate this sacred spot. They approached quietly and slowly with an attitude of awe and reverence. Because Jesus experienced desolation here, I am sure that these pilgrims found great comfort and consolation, great peace and joy, knowing that they were not alone with life's problems, but Jesus was with them.

The sun was appearing on the eastern horizon with the promise of a new day. As I moved about in the sunshine of his presence, I knew that my cry to the Father would never be one of despair, but one of victory, since Jesus is with me.

TWENTY-NINE

Sixth Word
"FATHER, INTO YOUR HANDS
I COMMEND MY SPIRIT."

Luke 23:44-46

Luke describes the death of Jesus in these words: "It was now around midday, and darkness came over the whole land until mid-afternoon with an eclipse of the sun. The curtain in the sanctuary was torn in two. Jesus uttered a loud cry and said: 'Father, into your hands I recommend my spirit.' After he said this, he expired."

Throughout his crucifixion Jesus never lost consciousness. He was fully conscious as he prayed Psalm 31:6. Jesus was familiar with this prayer. He added only one important word, "Father."

The verse, "Into your hands I commend my spirit" was part of a prayer which every Jewish mother taught her child to say as a night prayer. In our day, children are taught to say as a night prayer: "This night I lay me down to sleep." The Jewish mother taught her child to pray before the threatening dark came down: "Into your hands I commend my spirit."

As Jesus prayed this psalm, he was climaxing a

whole life of giving. He died as he had lived, with a prayer on his lips and a heart bent on fulfilling his Father's will perfectly.

Earlier in his public ministry at Jacob's Well, Jesus informed us: "Doing the will of him who sent me and bringing his work to completion is my food" (Jn 4:34).

How faithfully Jesus fulfilled what was foretold about him: "Behold I come; in the written scroll it is prescribed for me. To do your will, O my God, is my delight, and your law is within my heart!" (Ps 40:8-9).

And the psalmist tells us how Jesus was to fulfill the Father's will by announcing the Good News. Listen to his words:

> I announced your justice in the vast assembly;
>> I did not restrain my lips, as you, O Lord, know.
> Your justice I kept not hid within my heart;
>> Your faithfulness and your salvation I have spoken of;
> I have made no secret of your kindness
>> and your truth in the vast assembly."
>
> (Ps 40:10-11)

Jesus taught us how precious we would be to him if we all did the will of the Father. "Whoever does the will of God is brother and sister and mother to me" (Mk 3:35).

In the Sermon on the Mount, Jesus told us that our salvation depends upon our fulfilling the will of God in our lives. Listen to him say: "None of those who cry out, 'Lord, Lord' will enter the kingdom of

God but only the one who does the will of my
Father in heaven" (Mt 7:21).

Paul gives us some sage advice in his own characteristic way: "Do not conform yourselves to this age
but be transformed by the renewal of your mind, so
that you may judge what is God's will, what is
good, pleasing and perfect" (Rom 12:2).

And again: "Do not continue in ignorance, but
try to discern the will of the Lord" (Eph 5:17).

How pleasing must have been Jesus' submission
to the Father. Even on the cross Jesus died like a
child falling asleep in his father's arms.

Can I, with open hands and open mind and
heart, make this prayer of Jesus my own?

Test yourself by using the words of Brother
Charles of Jesus in his Prayer of Abandonment:

"Father, I abandon myself into your hands;
    do with me what you will—
Whatever you may do, I thank you—
I am ready for all, I accept all.

Let your will be done in me,
    and in all your creatures—
I wish no more than this, O Lord.

Into your hands I commend my soul;
I offer it to you with all the love of my heart,
and so need to give myself,
to surrender myself into your hands,
without reserve,
and with abundant confidence,
for you are my Father."

THIRTY

Seventh Word
"NOW IT IS FINISHED."

John 19:30

In this one brief statement from the cross Jesus says very much about himself. Even in death Jesus remains in perfect command of his destiny. Jesus himself pronounced the moment of his death. At this moment his work on earth would be accomplished.

Earlier in his ministry Jesus gave us the image of himself as the Good Shepherd. He told us that he loves us, his sheep, so much that he was willing to lay down his life for us. He made it quite clear that it was the free gift of himself, and that no human power could take his life from him. How concisely, yet how convincingly Jesus said: "No one takes it from me: I lay it down freely" (Jn 10:18).

Only John records the words of Jesus on the cross: "Now it is finished." The other evangelists tell us that Jesus "cried out with a loud voice." Both of these expressions are equally correct. In fact, they are expressing the same thought, for they come from the same Greek word.

This expression of Jesus was not a statement of weary defeat. On the contrary, it was a shout of triumph. It was a shout of joy because the victory was won. Jesus had brought his tremendous task to a triumphant conclusion.

In the eyes of the world, it looked like Jesus went down in defeat, and this cry might have seemed to come from a broken, dying victim. However, at that very moment the power of evil was broken, sin and death had been conquered, a world had been redeemed. Little wonder that Paul could cry out: "Oh death, where is your victory? Oh death, where is your sting?" (1 Cor 15:55).

It was early in the morning as I sat in the peaceful stillness of the chapel on Calvary. While I dared not break the hallowed stillness of early morning, I felt like shouting out with Jesus: "Yes, it is finished."

While no words crossed my lips, my heart burst forth with "thanks be to God, it is over, it is done!" The time of death is a very solemn moment and not to be fractured by any loud or disturbing noise, but the joy in my heart could not be stilled.

My heart kept singing in wordless repetition: "Thank you, Jesus. You did this all for me." I could well imagine the bursts of triumphant praise which reecho throughout the heavenly court.

In a vision, John heard the voices of many angels, living creatures and elders, countless in number, thousands and tens of thousands cry out:

"Worthy is the Lamb that was slain
to receive power and riches, wisdom and
strength
honor and glory and praise!" (Rv 5:12).

This hymn of praise is a perfect response to the victorious cry of Jesus: "Now it is finished!"

My reflection next turned to my own life. How paradoxical our life can become! When we look back from the vantage point of time, we can see more clearly how God's will was accomplished in our lives.

Perhaps in our lives there may have been some experiences which seemed at the time to be tragic. These experiences might have caused us some sorrow and disappointment, maybe even discouragement. However, after the lapse of time we can see what tremendous blessings these were, in disguise.

There might have been times when we were misunderstood, criticized, ridiculed, but eventually these, too, might have brought us untold benefits.

How plainly God spoke to us through Isaiah: "My thoughts are not your thoughts, nor are your ways my ways" (Is 55:8).

Jesus told us: "Whoever wishes to be my follower must deny his very self, take up his cross each day, and follow in my steps" (Lk 9:23).

If, with his help, we are faithful in accepting our daily cross, we can be assured of his response:

"Well done! You are an industrious and reliable servant. Since you were dependable in a small matter I will put you in charge of larger affairs. Come, share your master's joy" (Mt 25:21).

THIRTY-ONE

TRIUMPHANT ENTRY INTO JERUSALEM

Matthew 21:1-11

A small group of us wanted to retrace the steps of Jesus as he made his messianic entry into the Holy City. We walked over to the village of Bethphage which is located on the eastern slope of Mount Olivet. There we read the scriptural account of the triumphant entry of Jesus into Jerusalem. There in silence we spent some time in prayer contemplating this tremendous event of salvation history.

Next we formed a little procession, walked up the slope from Bethphage to the top of Mount Olivet, then proceded down past the Garden of Olives and entered the Holy City through the St. Stephen's gate.

As we walked along, we prayed, sang and reflected on what Jesus must have been thinking on that day long ago. I am sure that we encountered some of the same attitudes from people which Jesus experienced.

Along the way we met a number of little children

who had grown accustomed to these processions. Without hesitation some came dancing, skipping, and singing as they walked along with us. Others sat on steps and waved and shouted to us as we passed by. Many of them were chanting in their own inimitable way "Hosanna," with a peculiar Arabic accent.

We also passed a number of adults along our route. Most of them were gracious. They greeted us with a smile and a little nod of the head. Others just looked at us, their faces expressionless.

Then we encountered a policeman astride his horse. He glared at us as we passed by. A cynical smile played on his face. His countenance seemed to portray utter contempt for the memorial aspect of our pilgrimage.

Jesus must have encountered attitudes similar to these as he rode over the same route on his borrowed beast of burden. Jesus understood well his triumphant entry into the hostile camp of his enemies!

The disciples and followers of Jesus were loudly proclaiming him as king: "Tell the daughter of Zion your king comes to you without display...." Jesus knew that these followers were sincere in their praise of him. I thought of the little children following us. They, too, in their own way were crying out:

"Hosanna to the Son of David!
Blessed is he who comes in the name
  of the Lord!
Hosanna in the highest!"

Another kind of crowd also followed Jesus. These people either witnessed or heard about the raising of Lazarus to life. They were eager to see Jesus work other signs, or perhaps even to receive some healing or benefit from him themselves.

Some of this type might have been among the adults whom we passed along the way. Perhaps they recognized something sacred about our procession; perhaps they were curious. Perhaps there was a longing in their hearts for the kind of peace and joy which only Jesus could bring. They might have heard of the great prophet, but did not really know him and could not therefore believe in him.

The third class which witnessed that first Palm Sunday procession hated Jesus, and found in him a threat to themselves and to their way of life. They could have stopped the whole demonstration if they had dared.

I then thought of the unhappy officer of the law whom we had encountered. He did not radiate any joy. I felt certain that his heart knew no peace. The words of Jesus rang in my heart: "If only you had known the path to peace this day. . ." (Lk 19:42).

We ended our procession in the Church of St. Anne, just inside the Gate of St. Stephen. We decided to spend the next hour resting in the peaceful atmosphere of the church, pondering the journey we had just made. This reflection occurred to me:

The exalted, resurrected, risen Jesus is received in very much the same way today as he was two thousand years ago. His enemies continue to be indifferent to him, to ignore him, and even to hate him. Some follow Jesus for their own gain. They are

Christian in name only, because they "want to save their own souls." They are chiefly concerned about backing away from hell, and miss the joy of "going to heaven."

Others have come to know Jesus and to love him with all their hearts. Their main concern is to continue to establish a deeper, richer relationship with him, and to love him more intensely. How pleased Jesus is with such friends!

THIRTY-TWO

JESUS LAMENTS

Luke 19:41-44

On the western slope of the Mount of Olives, one can enjoy a magnificent view of Jerusalem with the whole city fully displayed before him. It is a gorgeous sight to behold.

When Jesus was making his triumphal entry into the Holy City on Palm Sunday, he came from the village of Bethphage up the eastern slope, and then began his descent down the western side of the Mount of Olives. As he came to a turn in the road the whole city came into view. Jesus stopped, gazed longingly and lovingly at the Holy City, and then shed bitter tears.

Jesus could foresee the fate which awaited Jerusalem. The Jews, with grandiose dreams of political power, were launching upon a course of intrigue which was going to lead to their destruction. Jesus knew what would happen. He had warned them many times. On an earlier occasion he had cried out: "O Jerusalem, Jerusalem . . . . How often have I wanted to gather your children together as a mother bird collects her young under her wings, and you refused me!" (Lk 13:34).

In the year 70 A.D., Jerusalem was destroyed. The

devastation was so thorough that a historian wrote that you could plough a furrow right through the middle of what had been the city of Jerusalem.

Jesus came to offer his people a way of life, a plan for peace, the joy of salvation; but they refused to accept him. When Jesus saw the useless pain and suffering, the death and destruction which was to befall them, he wept bitter tears of sorrow. How heartrending is his lament: "If only you had known the path to peace this day; but you have completely lost it to view" (Lk 19:42).

Jesus must have often reached out in love to the inhabitants of Jerusalem. The synoptic Gospels dwell a great deal on Jesus' ministry in Galilee, but John centers much of Jesus' teaching around the feasts in Jerusalem.

Nothing hurts so much as to offer our love to someone, only to be rejected and spurned. Life's bitterest tragedy is to give one's heart to someone, only to have it broken. Jesus knew that experience. He knows it still. What happened to Jesus in Jerusalem happens to him each day in our times. He still comes to us and we still reject him.

There is a beautiful church built on the slope of Mount Olivet to commemorate this experience of sorrow in the life of Jesus. It is called the Dominus Flevit Church—The Lord Wept. The building has an unusual shape. At first glance it looks almost like a huge tower, then the real artistry, the beauty, the magnificence and the message of the architect bursts upon the beholder. The architect has creatively and expertly designed it to look like an immense teardrop!

When you enter the Church you are struck by the window of clear glass over the altar table. It commands a panoramic view of the whole city, much as Jesus saw it on that day when he was so deeply moved.

As we were celebrating the Eucharist on this altar, the words of the psalmist kept coming back to me:

Pray for the peace of Jerusalem!
May peace be within your walls (Ps 122:6-7).

Jesus is living with us and within us. However, each day he comes anew in some fashion, to remind us of his presence and his indwelling. He may arrest our attention to observe the beauty of creation. He may reach out to us through a brother or sister whom we find hard to accept and love.

He may come bearing his cross in the guise of a person suffering physically, emotionally, or spiritually. He may come to us hungry, thirsty, homeless.

He may be asking us to abandon a program, a person, or a project which is leading us away from him. We may find that he is asking too much from us when he asks us to give up our own will and do things his way.

In his account of the Last Judgment, Jesus is asking us to love one another as we love him. He gives us this guarantee: "I assure you, as often as you did it for one of my least brothers, you did it for me" (Mt 25:40).

The night before he handed himself over to death he begged us: "Love one another as I have loved you" (Jn 15:12). The very next day he gave his life for us, so great was his love.

Does Jesus have any cause to weep over our world...over our city...over me?

THIRTY-THREE

JESUS UNDER FIRE

Matthew 21 and 22

During the season of Lent we try to come to know Jesus better. We simply cannot love a person we do not know. The better we know Jesus as a Person, the more we will be able to love him.

Throughout his public life Jesus revealed much about himself. A thousand adjectives cannot describe the many facets of his personality. There always remains that aura of other-worldliness about him. But it is a well-known fact that a person proves his real character when under stress and strain. So, Jesus teaches us much about himself and his personality as he deals with his enemies.

In Jerusalem, the Islamic Dome of the Rock has been built on the probable site of the ancient Jewish Temple. The Mosque is surrounded by a spacious area paved with huge flagstones. As I sat in this area one day, I thought I could see Jesus walking with his apostles among the people congregated here around the Temple. Here is the place where his enemies confronted him. Here in the precincts of the Temple they attacked him and tried to discredit him by posing difficult questions which they hoped would entrap him.

In dealing with his foes, Jesus shows his courage and strength. Here, as elsewhere, he rose majestically to every challenge his enemies could hurl at him.

His friends begged him not to go into this hostile territory where his life was threatened. However, Jesus was compelled to go. In the first place, the Father wanted him to bring the Good News, whatever the cost might be. Every man had to hear his message: Pharisees, Sadducees, Scribes, sinners, tax-collectors, prostitutes, gentiles — all, without exception.

Secondly, Jesus loved every person as his brother or sister. They were all children of the Father. He must risk using every possible means to win their stony hearts. He must continue to reach out in love, to the very end.

Jesus was fearless. He drove the money-changers from the Temple. "My house shall be called a house of prayer, but you are turning it into a den of thieves" (Mt 21:13). His parables struck at the root of the problem of his enemies. The parable of the tenants, the two sons, the wedding banquet: "The invited are many, the elect are few" (Mt 22:14). All this he said without apology, without any watering down. Jesus did not change one iota of the Father's message. He was not threatened by anyone or anything, because he had come to do the will of his Father.

Jesus did not defend himself. He spoke the truth, and the truth needs no defense. Nor did he wallow in self-pity when rejection came.

Under attack, Jesus manifests his loving concern for those to whom he was trying to minister, even though they did not believe in him. He demonstrates his determination to bring the Good News of salvation to all men, including his enemies.

Jesus also proved himself far superior to all those who challenged him, sometimes utterly devastating them as he responded to their objections. Yet, in spite of his firmness, he remained humble and gentle.

Under attack, Jesus proved himself a God of infinite compassion. He could have destroyed his enemies by a single act of his will, but he preferred to appear a total failure before men, hoping that this approach might touch their hardened hearts.

Jesus was aware of the intrigue, the plotting, the hatred which was moving in against him. He knew well that his time among his people was growing short, yet he fearlessly and lovingly continued to appeal to them.

Jesus was willing to accept apparent failure. He took no precautions to protect himself from personal harm. To the very end, he reached out in love. With tear-filled eyes, Jesus could say: "Oh Jerusalem, Jerusalem, murderess of prophets and stoner of those who were sent to you! How often have I yearned to gather your children, as a mother bird gathers her young under her wings, but you refused me" (Mt 23:37).

This is the mystery of love! This is the mystery of Jesus!

THIRTY-FOUR

CAVE OF BETRAYAL

Matthew 26:36-46

At the foot of the Mount of Olives is a large natural cave. This cave is venerated as the place where Jesus suffered his terrible agony and was betrayed by Judas. It is called the Cave of Betrayal or the Grotto of Gethsemane.

After the Last Supper, "Jesus went with them to a place called Gethsemane" (Mt 26:36). Here Jesus asked his disciples to spend time with him in prayer. He invited his three favorite apostles—Peter, John and James—to the innermost garden, and begged them to pray with him.

Overcome with fatigue and grief, they promptly fell asleep. Jesus realized that he was all alone in his dreadful agony, and the pain of loneliness intensified his suffering. Gently he reproached his apostles: "So you could not stay awake with me for even an hour?" (Mt 26:40).

As we were preparing to celebrate the Eucharist here in the Cave of Betrayal, a priest came in. He was all alone. He asked if he might concelebrate with us. We were delighted to have him. He was a missionary from Africa on his way home to his native Italy for rest and renewal. He spoke only a few words in English, but we were able to communicate a little.

In the homily, as I was speaking about the loneliness of Jesus in his hour of sorrow and distress, I saw tears flowing down the cheeks of my fellow-priest. He was lonely—lonely for his mission flock, lonely for his natural family as well as for his religious family in Italy. Furthermore, he was travelling all alone in Israel. He had no one with whom he could share his experience of the holy places.

Jesus experienced the pain of loneliness. At this crucial hour in his life, the Father seemed to have abandoned him, causing Jesus to cry out: "Abba (Oh Father), you have the power to do all things. Take this cup away from me" (Mk 14:36).

His apostles, too, abandoned him in this hour of need. They did not seem to sense the crisis he was suffering. They fell asleep. Jesus foresaw the denial of Peter, his chosen leader. He saw the perfidy of Judas, who was at that moment preparing to seek him out to betray him.

Jesus suffered the fear of the dreadful sufferings which lay ahead—the rejection, the scorn, the loneliness, the awful disgrace of crucifixion. Jesus experienced all this pain so that he might assuage our pain and our suffering.

At this moment Jesus craved human consolation, especially from his friends and close companions, but that was denied him. Jesus then turned to his Father in prayer. "In his anguish, he prayed with all the more intensity" (Lk 22:44). Thus Jesus once again teaches us much about prayer.

In the first place, prayer is our love relationship with our Father. Jesus found comfort and consolation only in his Father. He is thus encouraging us to turn to our loving Father in times of need.

Secondly, only in prayer was Jesus able to see clearly the will of the Father. It was while Jesus was absorbed in prayer that he was able to say: "My Father, if it is possible, let this cup pass me by. Still, let it be as you would have it, not as I" (Mt 26:39). Jesus was single-hearted. Only his Father's will mattered.

As we come close to our loving Abba in prayer, we will be able to see and comprehend to a greater extent his divine will in our lives. Prayer gives us a more cosmic view. It helps us to rise above self and say: "Your will be done."

Thirdly, while Jesus was at prayer, he experienced once again the infinite love which the Father has for him. Furthermore, Jesus looked beyond the confines of that garden and his heart burned with the intensity of his divine love for us.

Love cannot risk not giving. Love must give all without counting the cost. Jesus' love is so intense that he had to give all.

As that divine love welled up in his heart, it burned away the fear, the discouragement, the anxiety, the pain. His love compelled him to enter totally into the redemptive mystery.

That love gave him the strength and courage to say: "Get up! Let us be on our way! See, my betrayer is here" (Mt 26:46).

THIRTY-FIVE

JESUS AND JUDAS

John 18:1-14

In the Cave of Betrayal there are several large paintings depicting the events of the betrayal and arrest of Jesus. Over the main altar is a picture of Judas approaching Jesus. As I sat in the dimly-lit grotto one day all alone, I had an eerie feeling as I looked at the shadowy figure of Judas coming toward Jesus.

Feelings of disappointment, sorrow, anger, empathy crowded into my consciousness. However, soon the awareness of the great love of Jesus emerged like the noonday sun above all the intrigue, hatred, perfidy. Three special qualities of Jesus' love impressed themselves upon my mind:

Firstly, Jesus loved with a protective love. Listen to his plea to his captors: "If I am the one you want, let these men go" (Jn 18:8). This is characteristic of Jesus. He was not thinking about himself, but about others. He is always protecting, safeguarding his own.

I pondered momentarily how often I need to remind myself that he *does* love me. He loves me just as I am, with all my human weakness, my seldom-

used gifts, and my feeble attempts to respond to his
great love.

What reassurance Jesus gives me of his limitless
love when he says: "As the Father has loved me, so I
have loved you" (Jn 15:9). The Father's love is infinite; so is Jesus' love for me.

Yet in spite of this great love, how often I lack
trust! How prone I am to question God's will! The
disciple whom Jesus loved assures me again: "Love
has no room for fear; rather, perfect love casts out
all fear" (1 Jn 4:18).

Secondly, besides loving his friends, Jesus loved
those who were his enemies. The heart of Jesus must
have been broken by the traitorous act of Judas.
Jesus had called him into discipleship. He taught
him, he encouraged him, he loved him. How painful must have been this rejection by one of his own
chosen ones. How aptly the psalmist expresses it:

If an enemy had reviled me,
    I could have borne it:
If he who hates me had vaunted himself against
    me,
    I might have hidden from him.
But you, my other self,
    my companion and my bosom friend!
You, whose comradeship I enjoyed;
    at whose side I walked in procession in the
    house of God! (Ps 55:13-15).

Jesus accepted the hypocritical embrace of Judas.
He even permitted Judas to kiss him. Listen to the
final but loving appeal of Jesus to Judas: "Judas,

would you betray the Son of Man with a kiss?"
(Lk 22:48).

How often have I played the role of Judas? My
priorities get out of focus so easily. I get too busy to
give Jesus the time he asks of me. My concern for
self gets in his way all too frequently. My own will
becomes such an obstacle! The litany is endless.

As I think of Judas, I am aware that, but for the
grace of God, there go I. How grateful I am for the
compassion, the mercy which rescued me from
myself! How often he has swooped down with
eagle's wings to save me.

Thirdly, Jesus loves every person without exception. Jesus loves me. He told us, "I came that they
might have life and have it to the full" (Jn 10:10).
Even though my rebellious will and my weak human nature may entice me to deny him at times and
to betray him at other times, his love for me does
not change. It is immutable.

Jesus reminds us: "There is no greater love than
this: to lay down one's life for one's friends"
(Jn 15:13). Do we need further proof of his enduring love?

How correctly John says:

"Of his fullness
we have all had a share—
Love following upon love" (Jn 1:16).

THIRTY-SIX

JESUS ARRESTED

John 18:1-14

The Garden of Gethsemane is one of my favorite places of prayer. The Garden was within walking distance from the place where I lived for a time in Jerusalem. The grove of young olive trees offers a haven of semi-privacy, while the rustle of their small leaves forms background music for prayer.

The inviting seclusion of the Cave of Betrayal here in the Garden, offers comfort and protection if the weather becomes inclement. Here in the Cave the words of Jesus seem to reecho throughout the cavernous depths.

The Garden is one of my favorite places of prayer because here Jesus reveals so very much about himself — his personality, his character, his obedience, his love.

Jesus had courage. A powerful force of Roman soldiers and temple guards came to arrest him. They came "with lanterns, torches and weapons," even though the full moon would light their way. They apparently came prepared to seek out Jesus in case he should be hiding among the caverns.

Far from hiding, Jesus "stepped forward," faced

them courageously and said: "Who is it you want?"
The arresting party must have been startled at his
unexpected show of courage. "Jesus the Nazarean,"
they replied. Without hesitation he identified himself: "I am he."

Jesus remains entirely in command of the situation. As Jesus identified himself, the arresting party
"retreated slightly and fell to the ground." Judas the
betrayer stands by helplessly. Whether this recoil-
ing of the guards was due to the courage and calm
presence of Jesus before them, or whether their
reaction was an unconscious recognition of his
divine majesty, we can never be certain.

Jesus continued to baffle them. He demonstrated
not only his divine power but also his loving concern as he healed the ear of Malchus, a slave of the
high priest.

By proving his authority and power, Jesus was
making a final attempt to win the hearts of these
men. Even though they were only servants and soldiers under orders, he tried to reach out to touch
their hearts once again. We will never know how
some of these men must have been affected by his
majestic presence and power.

Another point to ponder is how Jesus once again
showed his single-mindedness in doing the will of
his Father. Nothing else really made any difference
to him. Whatever the Father asked: that was sufficient for Jesus.

He had assured us earlier in his life that he was
the Good Shepherd who would lay down his life for
us, his sheep.

"The Father loves me for this:
  I lay down my life
  to take it up again.
No one takes it from me;
  I lay it down freely
I have the power to lay it down
  and I have the power to take it up again
This command I received from my Father."
  (Jn 10:17-18).

When the moment finally came for Jesus to lay down his life, his human nature rebelled, but in prayer he found the courage to empty himself totally. Listen to his prayer: "Father, if it is your will, take this cup from me; yet not my will but yours be done" (Lk 22:42).

How true are the words the sacred writer put into Jesus' mouth: "I have come to do your will, Oh God" (Heb 10:7).

And how appropriate this other reflection, from Hebrews: "Son though he was, he learned obedience from what he suffered; and when perfected, he became the source of eternal salvation for all who obey him" (Heb 5:8-9).

How perfectly Jesus lived out the prayer he had given to us: "Your will be done on earth as it is in heaven" (Mt 6:10).

THIRTY-SEVEN

JESUS ON TRIAL

John 18:28-19:16

In this land of our exile blighted by sin, many travesties of justice take place. Deplorable and cruel as these may be, there is no greater miscarriage of justice than the trial of Jesus.

Man not only dared to sit in judgment on his God, but even to find his God guilty of death. In spite of such an infamous, blasphemous condemnation, God turned this injustice into the redemptive act which saved the world.

I was sitting alone in the lower level of the Ecce Homo Hostel. This is the area of the Lithostrotos or the judgment seat of Pilate. Today huge thick flagstones still form the pavement area. These stones are striated to prevent the horses of the Roman soldiers from slipping.

As I sat there on a wooden bench, I began to reflect on those who sat in judgment of Jesus.

Jesus was first brought before Caiaphas and the Sanhedrin. These men who once held supreme power in Israel exercised the little power that remained to them under the Roman domination. The spectacle was disgraceful. They resorted to deceit. They broke the covenant that God had made with them. They violated their own laws.

The second person to sit in judgment on Jesus was Herod. This puppet ruler had rejected the covenant long ago. Jesus was no threat to him, as he was to the Jewish leaders. Herod was an uncaring person. The appearance of Jesus before him was a joke to Herod. He treated Jesus like a fool.

Next, Jesus was brought before Pilate, who had the real power and authority. How Pilate abused that power! Pilate turned coward. He wanted to appease the crowd. At the same time he wanted to turn the deceit of the Jews back on themselves. He exploited the situation, and Jesus became his pawn. Pilate forgot that Jesus was a person and used the occasion as a vindictive political maneuver.

Throughout these mock trials, Jesus remained silent. He did not offer one word in defense of himself. He answered only those questions which his judge had a right to ask.

How that silence must have infuriated his accusers! It turned the guilt and responsibility back on themselves. How eloquently his silence spoke to them of their cunning deceit, their insane jealousy, their vile hatred!

Jesus was flogged, crowned with thorns, clothed in a purple robe to be mocked as a king. When Pilate presented Jesus to the bloodthirsty crowd with the words: "Look at the man!" Jesus' silence must have touched many hearts. It angered some. It caused others to wonder. Still others must have regretted what was happening, and must have deeply deplored their own participation in the dreadful proceedings.

Today, risen, exalted, glorified, Jesus stands before another court. It is made up of all his creatures throughout the world who are totally dependent upon his love. He sustains them at every moment of life.

Yet the court of pseudo-science would banish him from the universe. This court of proud technocracy, so sufficient unto itself, has set up its own plastic and neon gods.

The court of self-indulgent pleasure-seekers has condemned Jesus for restricting their freedom. His silence annoys them as it pricks their consciences. They maintain that Jesus is dead. The world no longer needs him, they say.

Jesus' silence makes me look at myself. He does not judge me, but his silence forces me to judge myself.

Do I honestly, sincerely, enthusiastically fully accept his words? Do I let them become a way of life for me? Do his words complicate my life? His silence will force me to sit in judgment on my own way of life. It provokes the truth from me.

His silence makes me look at my self-centeredness, at the ulterior motives which spur me into action.

His silence also tells me that he knows that I am his disciple striving to walk in his footsteps, even though it be at some distance. His silence tells me that he is happy I am striving.

THIRTY-EIGHT

Holy Thursday
"I HAVE GREATLY DESIRED TO EAT THIS PASSOVER WITH YOU"

Luke 22:7-20

I was fortunate in arriving at the Cenacle in late afternoon. I wanted to spend some of the early evening hours there so that my stay would coincide with the time of day when Jesus and his apostles gathered for the Last Supper.

It was a warm sunny afternoon as I climbed the steps to the Upper Room. This building is now owned by the people of Israel. They permit pilgrims to visit this shrine, sacred to all Christians, but they do not permit any religious service there except for a paraliturgical ceremony on Pentecost Sunday.

I wanted to be alone in the Cenacle to try to recapture what took place here on the first Holy Thursday evening. It was very quiet at this time of the day with only a few visitors dropping in. I made myself a comfortable seat on the floor against the wall.

In the stillness I could almost hear Jesus say to his beloved apostles: "I have greatly desired to eat this

Passover with you before I suffer" (Lk 22:15).

It must have been a joyous occasion for Jesus because he was about to give them and us the unfathomable eucharistic gift of himself. Jesus had promised to remain with us, but it would be so easy for us to forget his spiritual indwelling. He gave us a more tangible sign of his presence under the appearances of bread and wine.

We can well imagine how the heartbeats of the apostles quickened as Jesus said: "This is my body," and "This cup is the new covenant in my blood."

I doubt if Jesus could conceal his own excitement about this gift of himself. His voice with all its masculine tenderness must have betrayed him. Then Jesus ordained his apostles as his first priests by commissioning them to continue what he had just done: "Do this as a remembrance of me."

How hallowed and how sacred this evening must have been for the apostles, for priests throughout the world and for all Christendom! Even the foreboding of what tomorrow might bring was far removed at this sacred moment.

There was one cloud, however, which Jesus could not dissipate. Jesus described it in this way: "And yet the hand of my betrayer is with me at this table" (Lk 22:21). This expression of Jesus was more an appeal to Judas than a lament. How often Jesus had reached out to Judas in love, but Judas was not listening. Jesus knew that it was far better to love and be hurt than not to love at all. Furthermore, his divine love could not exclude anyone.

As the evening shadows began to fall I could well imagine Judas slipping off into the dark to carry out his insidious plan. The evangelist writes: "No sooner had Judas eaten the morsel than he went out." Then he adds this awesome note: "It was night" (Jn 13:30). It was night in the streets of Jerusalem. It was night in the heart of Judas for he had shut out the Light.

From that Cenacle on the first Holy Thursday evening, that directive coming from the lips of Jesus was beamed around the world for all times: "Do this as a remembrance of me."

Today, nearly two thousand years later, some priest somewhere in the world is pronouncing those same words at this very moment. Every few seconds a new eucharistic celebration is beginning.

Imagine the paean of praise, thanks, and glory that is being offered to the Father at every moment of every day. Jesus is forever uniting his prayer with ours in the Eucharist, and presenting our prayer to the Father.

That is why, even though the intrigue, the plotting, and the hatred was moving in on Jesus, he could rejoice to offer the Eucharist with his apostles. His words ring true when he said: "I have greatly desired to eat this Passover with you before I suffer" (Lk 22:15).

Today when we gather to offer the Eucharist, though we number few or many, we are united with all our brothers and sisters around the whole world to offer our praise and thanksgiving to our loving Father. In each Mass we are united with the whole Body of Jesus, raising our hearts and our voices in prayer to God.

Each time we come together to offer the Eucharist, Jesus joins us as our eternal highpriest, and each time, he says to us: "I have greatly desired to eat this Passover with you."

It was time to leave the Cenacle. I still felt a little sad that I was not able to offer the Eucharist in this hallowed spot. However, the thought that Mass at this very moment was being offered around the world filled my heart with joy.

THIRTY-NINE

Good Friday
CRUCIFIXION AND
DEATH OF JESUS

John 19:17-37

Good Friday is a special day of remembering for every Christian. On memorial days we like to go back in memory or spirit to the event we are recalling. We even like to revisit the commemorative place if possible.

Today, let us go in spirit to revisit Calvary. As we climb that rocky ledge, let us sit on its summit and recall the powers which clashed on this height.

A human power grossly abused robbed Jesus of his life, but from that death issued a power to save a world. There is much pathos on Calvary. Here Jesus was abandoned by his friends and rejected by his own people. Unaware of the tremendous conflict being waged with other-worldly spirits, the soldiers cast lots for his garments. Their selfish concerns blinded them to the mystery which was taking place before their very eyes.

His enemies' hatred and fear did not diminish, but grew in intensity until the bitter end. They gave vent to their fear by their relentless blasphemy, insults, mockery, and derision.

Yet on the other hand there is awe, wonder, reverence on Calvary's hill. There is awe in the heart of the centurion; others beat their breasts. The holy women stood in reverence.

Since the death of Jesus on the cross there is a sacredness about death. It is a time of separation and sorrow for the human heart. Pain and sorrow are different from melancholy and depression. There is a sacredness about death because there is always a presence — a divine presence. Death is a doorway into an eternal union with the Father.

In the Christian heart there is no place for sadness even though there is sorrow. There is no room for depression because of the truth we are contemplating — the crucifixion and death of Jesus. His death gives meaning to death. His death brings a joy and peace to death even though there is sorrow.

Our contemplation on the crucifixion of Jesus should move us into a deep spirit of gratitude. We are grateful to the degree that we appreciate a gift. If we know that a gift costs the giver much sacrifice and effort, our gratitude increases in proportion. Jesus said: "There is no greater love than this: to lay down one's life for one's friends" (Jn 15:13). Our gratitude, then, for what Jesus did for us should know no bounds.

Calvary moves us into a great spirit of compassion. When we pause to reflect on the price which Jesus paid for our sins, it should give us a willingness and a readiness to suffer with and for others. Jesus lives in his body today. We should be moved to reach out in compassion for the suffering members of his body. Jesus said: "I assure you, as often as you did it for one of my least brothers, you did it for me" (Mt 25:40). This consideration should move us to a great spirit of compassion.

The death of Jesus on the cross would inflame our love for him. Love is mutual. Love is reciprocal. A spurned love wounds deeply. Jesus himself assures us that there is no greater love than this. How great must be the love with which we reciprocate! Can we afford to be niggardly with a love which has been given so abundantly?

Jesus had still another gift to give. He promised us: "I will not leave you orphaned; I will come back to you" (Jn 14:18). Jesus remains with us through his Spirit. The Holy Spirit is the fullness of Jesus dwelling within us. Jesus explained it in this way: "I will ask the Father and he will give you another Paraclete to be with you always" (Jn 14:16).

John records that this is precisely what Jesus did when he died on the cross. "Then he bowed his head, and delivered over his spirit" (Jn 19:30). Now that Jesus is glorified, his Spirit reigns in our hearts.

Recall that at the beginning of Jesus' public ministry, at one of the feasts in the temple, he promised his spirit, as the living waters welling up within us. John records it in these words:

On the last and greatest day of the festival
    Jesus stood up and cried out:
'If anyone thirsts, let him come to me;
    let him drink who believes in me.
Scripture has it: From within him rivers of living
    water shall flow.'

And John adds this explanation: "Here he was referring to the Spirit whom those that came to believe in him were to receive. There was, of course, no Spirit as yet, since Jesus had not yet been glorified" (Jn 7:37-39).

The sufferings and death of Jesus were his glorification. On Calvary the gift of the Spirit became a reality.

Before we leave the hill of Calvary may our prayer be:

Lord, increase my gratitude,
    deepen my compassion,
    inflame my love.

FORTY

Holy Saturday
JESUS IN THE TOMB

Matthew 27:57-61

Close to the Shrine of the Holy Sepulchre is the Coptic Chapel, and also the Armenian Chapel. These are spacious rooms and contain many rock tombs dating from the time of Christ. The tombs are open and a person may walk into them even though the entrance is quite low. These tombs are called the Tombs of Nicodemus and Joseph of Arimathea, since scripture tells us that Joseph owned a tomb in this garden.

When I arrived in these chapels, there was semidarkness and an emptiness about them. This same atmosphere must have prevailed around the tomb of Jesus on the first Good Friday night and throughout Holy Saturday.

After Jesus died, the gospels relate how reverently and courageously Joseph of Arimathea and Nicodemus buried the body of Jesus in the new tomb.

Imagine the feelings of all those present when Joseph "rolled a huge stone across the entrance of the tomb and went away." In our prayer, let us try to imagine what went on in the hearts of those who were closely associated with Jesus.

"Mary Magdalene and the other Mary remained sitting there, facing the tomb." There must have been a great emptiness in Mary Magdalene's heart. She loved Jesus intensely. Now he was gone. While she might have had some feelings of relief that his sufferings were over, she must have had a great feeling of loneliness. There were so few who understood her and her conversion.

The emptiness was augmented by the fact that Mary Magdalene was not expecting Jesus to rise from the dead. On the day of the resurrection, she thought that his body had been stolen. Furthermore, she did not recognize Jesus' voice when he asked: "Woman, why are you weeping?" It was only when Jesus called her by name that she recognized him.

The apostles were still very much frightened. They must have been filled with sorrow and regret that they had abandoned Jesus in his most critical hour. I am sure that some of them regretted that they did not die with him. They were just beginning to experience the emptiness of life without him.

What a void must have been in the heart of Peter! His sorrow must have bordered on remorse as he reflected on his own weakness and his total disregard for the warning that Jesus had given him.

Likewise, the disciples on the road to Emmaus revealed not only their own feelings of disappointment in the death of Jesus, but they must have reflected the sentiments of many other disciples when they said: "We were hoping that he was the one who would set Israel free" (Lk 24:21). The crucifixion and death of Jesus shattered all their dreams of restoring the glory of Israel.

The guards stationed at the tomb may have been the most unfeeling group. They were hired to do a job which they did not understand. They may have regarded their task as ridiculous: who would disturb a buried corpse? The day must have dragged on for them, while the night seemed interminable. I wondered what they thought and felt after the resurrection!

How did Mary, the Mother of Jesus, feel? Her heart must have found some relief knowing that the inhuman treatment of her Son was over. She might have had some vague notion that her Son would come again. Surely she lived with some expectancy.

It is not likely that she knew with any degree of clarity that Jesus would rise gloriously from the tomb. If she did, I am sure she would have brought that comfort and consolation to the apostles and the holy women. If she had been able to do so, they would not have been taken by such complete surprise on the day of the resurrection.

If we could have made a survey on the first Holy Saturday while Jesus remained in the tomb, I am sure that we would have found many different reactions. Common to all, however, must have been a deep feeling of emptiness.

As I sat there in the semidarkness, facing the empty tombs, I wondered what our life would be like without the presence of Jesus with us and within us, without his presence in his Word, without his presence in the Eucharist.

FORTY-ONE

Easter Sunday
RESURRECTION JOY

John 16:20

The resurrection of Jesus from the dead, and all that it implies, fills us with great joy. How joyously we sing our Alleluia!

These days we are striving to capture the deep, quiet joy which must have filled the heart of our Blessed Mother as she rejoiced with her risen Son!

Today we hear Mary Magdalene joyously shouting "Rabbouni!" when she recognized Jesus resurrected and real. How appropriately she called him Teacher, for he had taught her much about God's love for her, and he also taught her how to respond in love.

What joy must have filled the hearts of the apostles and all his disciples. Thomas surely expressed the sentiments of all when he exclaimed "My Lord and my God!"

The Resurrection is a time of joy because all the promises and prophecies, all the hopes and expectations of the Old Testament are fulfilled.

It is a time of great rejoicing because, by his rising from the dead, Jesus gives meaning to our life of exile. It ends our alienation from God and promises us a life of genuine happiness in a perfect union with God our Father.

We rejoice because we realize that we are not walking the pathway of life alone. Jesus is alive. He is with us personally and individually more fully, more completely than ever before in human history.

We are filled with joy because Jesus is with us assisting us, encouraging us, strengthening us for every task in life.

We are joyous and filled with genuine Christian joy because we know that Jesus suffered all the pain, the sorrow, the hardships which are our lot in life. He is with us as our healer, our redeemer, our savior.

This is precisely why Jesus revealed the Good News to us, so that we can be a joyous people. He said:

"All this I tell you
   that my joy may be yours
   and your joy may be complete" (Jn 15:11)

Jesus is calling us to be a people of joy. Too long have we been merely crucifixion Christians rather than resurrection Christians. Too seldom have we radiated the real Christian joy which should be ours.

There is so little joy in the world because we have not come to the only authentic source of joy: the Good News of God's love for us, proved so concretely by the rising of Jesus from the dead. He could not leave us. His love for us is so great that he had to devise a way of remaining with us and within us.

Genuine Christian joy is not a perpetual state of ecstatic hilarity. By no means! True joy is that interior peace and happiness which comes from our awareness that God loves us just as we are with all our human weaknesses, faults and failures. It comes also from the knowledge that we are striving in our own human way to respond to his infinite love.

There will be times when we will have to smile through our tears. There can be no crown without a cross. Jesus proved that.

Jesus tried to prepare us and show us that suffering is not incompatible with joy. He said:

"I tell you solemnly,
    you will be weeping and wailing
    while the world will rejoice;
    you will be sorrowful,
    but your sorrow will turn to joy" (Jn 16:20).

Listen to Paul's exhortation: "Rejoice in the Lord always! I say it again, Rejoice. . . The Lord is near" resurrected and living within us. (Phil 4:4).

And Paul prays for this blessing:

"May the God of hope fill you with joy
    and peace in your faith,
    That by the power of the Holy Spirit,
    your whole life and outlook
    may be radiant with hope" (Rom 15:13).

If our focus is always on Jesus, if our heart is assured of his love, then we will be joyous, then we will be able to LOOK REDEEMED.